Good Nights Now

Stephanie Donaldson-Pressman
Dr. Robert Pressman
Rebecca Jackson

Authors of *Matilda & Maxwell* ™

GoodParentGoodChild ™

For information:
Good Parent, Inc., One Regency Plaza, Providence, RI 02903.

A GoodParentGoodChild™ Book
ISBN-10 098321834X
ISBN-13 9780983218340

Cover photo: ©2011 Shutterstock
Author photo: Sara Zarrella Photography, LLC
Cover design: Lise Holliker Dykes
Character illustrations: Lou Jacque
Book design and composition: Anette Schuetz

CONTENTS

Stephanie Donaldson-Pressman, LICSW

Stephanie Donaldson-Pressman is a licensed clinical social worker and an internationally recognized author and trainer in the field of family therapy. Her ground-breaking text, *The Narcissistic Family: Diagnosis and Treatment*, introduced an entirely new diagnostic paradigm and an innovative therapeutic model for understanding and treating adults from emotionally abusive or neglectful families.

Stephanie is well known for her work with military families, and is a principal in the documentary film *Brats: Our Journey Home*. She has been an adjunct professor of psychology and family studies at the University of Rhode Island and the Community College of Rhode Island. She is bi-lingual and provides family and individual treatment to child, adolescent, and adult patients. The grandmother of three, Mimi enjoys writing nonsense stories and songs to entertain them!

Rebecca Jackson

Rebecca began working part-time for a pediatric psychology practice after the birth of her daughter. She has a 2½ year old daughter, Hunter Olivia, and a 12 year old step-son, Bobby. As the mother of both a toddler and a 'tween, she understands the unique challenges of parenting children of disparate ages. The "Mommy's Perspective" found throughout the book is meant to provide parents with thoughtful, caring tips to assist them.

Robert M. Pressman, Ph.D.

Dr. Robert Pressman is a pediatric psychologist, in practice for over 35 years. He is board certified in family and couples psychology by the American Board of Professional Psychology. He is the author of several landmark books and a co-author, with Stephanie Donaldson-Pressman, of *The Narcissistic Family: Diagnosis and Treatment.*

Dr. Pressman is the grandfather of three children. Besides just being with them, he enjoys hopping up and down with 30 month old Hunter, going on mystery trips with 11 year old Emma, taking 12 year old Bobby to ball games, and being called Pop-Pop.

ACKNOWLEDGMENTS

There are three authors of this book, and many people who were very helpful along the way.

In the beginning, however, there was one woman with a vision: Rebecca Jackson came to Robert and me in June, 2010 with the idea for a company—GoodParent, Inc.—that would publish books helpful to parents looking to solve one particular problem at a time. Out of that first meeting, the GoodParentGoodChild series was born. We, quite literally, owe it all to Rebecca. You never cease to amaze and delight us with your creativity, intelligence, humor, and generosity. Thank you for this amazing gift!—SDP and RMP

We are incredibly grateful to Alyssa Sullivan, friend and publicist extraordinaire, for the many hats that she wore during this process, for believing in the project from day one, and for teaching us about "hall running!" She has been a source of unwavering support and invaluable advice.

To all of the good parents in our practice who allowed us into the lives of their families, and took us along on the journey with them: we could not have written this without you.

On the technical side, we had a brilliant editor, Charlene Nichols, and a wonderful book designer Anette Schuetz. They made our jobs so much easier! Thanks, also, to the legal team of Meredith Ainbinder, Nicole Rizzo Smith, and Lisa Fleming of Sunstein, Kann, Murphy and Timbers who enthusiastically embraced the concept and were helpful in myriad ways. Lest we forget, it is Dennis Sousa, our computer technician, whose exquisite expertise and availability to quickly resolve or avoid unexpected glitches has made the production of this book possible.

Our gratitude to Lou Jacque cannot be overstated. This talented artist provided the author caricatures with humor and dedication, blizzards notwithstanding. Thanks, Lou.

[RPJ] Special thanks to my wonderful parents for their love, support and belief in the project. I can't thank you enough for all that you do for my family—the list is simply too long! Please know how much I appreciate you.

Many thanks to my terrific sister in-laws, Carol and Kim, for help with childcare and hotel rooms during this process. And always, with much love to my sister and brother, who make every family occasion a fun one.

[RMP] Drs. Judith and Donald Smith, are the authors of *Child Management: A Program for Parents and Teachers*, published in the late 1960's; this book has been a resource for me since its publication. It was Dr. Frank Greene, my mentor at Syracuse University, who introduced me to this book and to family therapy concepts that have become an integral part of my practice. Thank you.

[SDP] To Donna Musil, who kept nagging me about, "When are you going to write another book?" and to all the friends and family who have been put off and cancelled out on, while I tried to meet deadlines: I hope you now think it was worth it!

Overview

CONGRATULATE YOURSELF! We believe that you have chosen to focus on the single most important and life-altering opportunity in a child's life—experiencing a truly good night: going to bed on time, feeling safe and comfortable in his or her room for the entire night, and accomplishing this without fuss or drama. Once you, good parent, have helped your good child to master this challenge, all others will seem much easier.

Good Night will give you the insight, tools, and confidence to change your child's behavior. You will learn how these changes help your child feel safe, secure, loved, and proud. The techniques revealed in this book will give you a sense of empowerment and your child a sense of accomplishment. Good Night is written by three individuals with different skills, each with his or her unique perspective on parenting: Dr. Robert Pressman, a pediatric psychologist, in practice for over 35 years; Stephanie Donaldson-Pressman, a licensed clinical social worker and best-selling author; Rebecca Jackson, a mother of both a toddler and a tween.

Setting the Stage

Every family goes through rough spots—no matter how perfect they may seem to their co-workers, friends, relatives, bosses, or members of their religious community. Stephanie tells us about a patient who—no matter what problem her children present, or how extremely well she handles it—always introduces the drama *du jour* with, "Well, here I am again. The worst mother of the year!" She is absolutely positive that her neighbors are judging her and finding her parenting skills not "up to snuff," because *they* all have perfect lives with perfect children. At least, from the outside, that's how it looks.

As parents and therapists, we can assure you that, in truth, there are no perfect parents who always know, say, and do the most appropriate thing at exactly the right time. There also are no perfect children. Thank goodness for that! Were these perfect beings to exist, they would cause the rest of us to feel even more inadequate than we frequently feel.

Most of us are well-meaning, caring adults who want our children to get through the more-or-less 18-year period between birth and adulthood relatively unscathed. We know that our children will experience unhappiness, frustration, failure, rejection, illness, and heartbreak; we just hope that they also know joy, acceptance, love, success, confidence, and pride in the people they are becoming. As parents we wish to provide them with the tools to progress from childhood to adulthood with self-confidence and the knowledge that they have skills they can rely on to solve their own problems.

That confidence—and those skills—are not acquired easily. They happen through trial and error, mistakes made and learned from, and injuries (both physical and emotional) sustained and overcome. All of you suffer at least as much as your child every step and misstep along the way.

When It's Good, It's Very, Very Good...

Sometimes, you are really focused, insightful, helpful, and understanding. Those days, you *know* that you are a good parent and that your child has benefited enormously from your love, support, and wisdom. Those are the Good Days. Cherish them.

When It's Bad, It's Awful!

Then, there are the other days. Those are the days when you're tired, have a killer headache, or find out that the bank returned eight of your checks at $30.00 per check. Those are the days when you discover the bank deposit on the floor of your car, under a sippy cup filled with a mystery liquid that might, perhaps, once have been apple juice.

Those are the days when you FINALLY get the colicky baby to sleep and your 6 year old throws a fit about the no-cookies rule, slams the door, and wakes up the baby.

Or the days when your friend from high school is coming over for the first time in 10 years and you have exactly four hours to go grocery shopping, put it all away, clean the house (at least the downstairs), get the kids bathed and fed, take a shower and do your hair, find an outfit that looks reasonably becoming and doesn't have a food stain on it, uncork the wine, and defrost the "homemade" goodies you will casually offer her.

On that day, your 4 year old—who hasn't allowed you to sleep through the night without at least two intrusions and climbing in bed with you since he was 18 months old—decides to stage a protest of epic proportions in the checkout line because he cannot live without the bubble gum balls displayed prominently before him. You know it's wrong—you hate to do it—but you buy him the gum so you can just get out of the store!

And then you are so mad at both him and yourself that you don't like either of you very much. You put him in his car seat a bit roughly, and he complains, and you give him the death stare, and he starts to cry, and you think, "I'll give you something to cry about!" as you slam the car door. And, of course, it goes downhill from there. Those are the Dreadful Days. We all have them; we can't forget them, and we vow to never, ever let things get so out of hand again. Right?

Real Parents + Real Children = Real Problems

Naturally, it would be great if all days were Good Days. Perhaps in some universe far from our own, they are. In our universe, however, there are simply too many complications, stressors, conflicts, imperatives, rules, and conditions with which parents have to deal. We try so hard to be supportive and to give our children every possible advantage that it seems as if the little twits should be much better behaved and more appreciative than they are! After all, we are doing everything we can to ensure that their lives are safe, enriched, and full of experiences, toys, gadgets, eleven pairs of sneakers, etc.; you name it, we get it or do it. We do not want our babies to experience any kind of pain.

And that, good parent, is exactly how and why this book came to be written. In the midst of all our parenting "must do's," we have been so concerned about our child's comfort that we have forgotten about her need to learn to take care of herself, by herself. The ability to have a calm, pleasant bedtime routine followed by a night spent in her own room is one of the greatest gifts you can give to your daughter; it will mean more to your son than the absolutely coolest sneakers he will ever own. And, for you, good parent, it will be the gift of sleep—hours of unbroken sleep, without drama, demands, tears, or the presence of a child in your bed.

It's a Matter of Degree

As you will read later in the book when Rebecca weighs in with her "Mommy's Perspective," bedtime problems happen gradually, over time. It isn't as if a parent looks at her/his newborn and decides, I'm going to let this precious child disrupt my life, cause tension in the house, ruin my sleep every single night, and present behavioral challenges at school and at home for the next eight or ten or twelve years. Mommy and Daddy just love you so much!

It happens step by step. For example, Buddy has asthma, so Dad brings him into his bed to monitor him. Kira's grandmother comes to stay for six weeks, so she is given Kira's room and Kira sleeps with Mom and Dad; she starts on a mat on the floor, but ends up in the bed. Marshall has a new baby sister, and she gets to stay in a bassinette in Mommy's room; Marshall feels left out, so Mom and Dad just decide to do the family bed thing until the baby is...19?

By the time Mom and/or Dad have had it with the crowded bed, Buddy, Kira, and Marshall are there to stay. Getting them out and into their own rooms is a nightly ordeal that can go on for hours—with the child usually ending up back in the parents' bed—and the kids aren't all that well-behaved in the daytime, either. Sound familiar?

Back to the Top

Again, congratulate yourself! When you chose this book, you chose wisely. Within these pages, we present a technique which we refer to as What's the Rule?; deciding to give it a try is one of the best choices you have made for your family. You want to have peaceful evenings. You want to have well-behaved children. You want a quiet house at night. You want...Good Nights. You can have them, with some added bonuses thrown in for free.

Your child's experience of sleeping through the night in his own room will make him a happier, better behaved boy. Your daughter's teacher will notice how much more focused she seems, and how obedient and pleasant she is. Your children will be more polite and respectful with you and generally easier to deal with when you are trying to come up with solutions for other problem times—like getting up and ready for school or getting homework done without hassles. (FYI: Those are topics covered in other books in this series.)

What's the Rule? works. We also have a companion book for children, *Matilda and Maxwell's Good Night*. It's a fun book for you to read to your child, or for your child to read to you. It introduces this technique to children in a way that will both entertain and reassure them. The illustrations are wonderful; this book will quickly become one of your child's favorites!

Let's Get Organized

The book is divided into four parts. We want to make navigating the subject matter as easy as possible, so that you can pick a section that interests you, quickly find and read it. You don't have to wade through other information that, while interesting and of value, is not what you want to learn about at the moment.

Learning about "The 'Why' Behind 'How You Got Here'" in Part One, will put to rest (pardon the pun) any feelings of guilt or doubt that you may have regarding past experiences and failures with bedtime and bedtime routines for your children.

Once you understand and implement Part Two, "What's the Rule? Everything You Want to Know," you will see the end of those agonizing nights filled with temper tantrums and tears.

The material in Part Three, "All Kinds of Interesting Things You Need to Know," is helpful in sorting out all manner of everyday interactions between you and your child; you will immediately be able to use what you learn in this section.

Part Four, "Obstacles, Achievements, and Your Questions," includes case stories illustrating special circumstances that you will find fascinating; these are people with whom you can relate—good parents who make mistakes but care enough to explore new options in order to help their families. The final chapter, "Just the FAQ's" contains scenarios and concrete advice about what to do in unexpected, totally random, unique or once-in-a-lifetime situations. If you can think of it and it relates to bedtime, it's almost certainly in here.

About Our Stories

There are many case stories in this book; they're a lot more interesting to read than a bunch of facts. They also give a sense of reality to what we are describing. These are not picture-perfect parents with cookie-cutter kids; they are actual people who are facing the same challenges you are. Each of them had the ability to make bedtime a special, calm, and happy time in their day. All of these good parents ultimately tried What's the Rule? to deal with their nighttime problems. Every one of them had success. Why wouldn't you?

We recommend that you begin using the system as soon as possible. The only thing standing between you and a calm evening and a good night's sleep is, well, you—and how soon you start What's the Rule?

PART ONE

WHO You Are, WHERE You Are, AND HOW You Got Here

CHAPTER ONE

What's It All About?

Dr. Pressman

Mommy
Rebecca

Stephanie
LICSW

Three Voices: One Goal

The goal is to teach parents a simple, proven method to solve the bedtime problems they are experiencing with their children.

Is That Even Possible?

We know that *you* know that short of the use of manacles or the intervention of Super Nanny, your nighttime situation is probably beyond repair. You've tried everything, and nothing works. Or, it seems to work—for a couple of nights, then it's back to same old, same old. So will this technique really be any better?

In a Word, "Yes!"

Just flip through the Table of Contents and you're bound to think that this book just might have the answers you've been looking for. From "Who You Are, Where You Are, and How You Got Here," through the complete three chapter section devoted to What's the Rule? we take you on a step-by-step journey to realize the ease—and potential—of this technique. The final part, "Obstacles, Achievements and Your Questions," takes you into the lives of real families who have used this system effectively and answers any special questions you may have. This particular journey will end with your ability to establish a unique bedtime routine, thoughtfully designed for your family. You and your children will finally be able to enjoy your nights together—and apart: each of you in your own room, all night. Along the way, you will learn "All Kinds of Interesting Things Good Parents Need to Know!" Sounds pretty good, doesn't it?

Nights in My House Are Too Hard!

Bedtime is often the first major parenting challenge in families. It is also one of the more important ones. Throughout the book, we demonstrate the technique called What's the Rule? using real families—with real problems. We realize that knowing that other families have struggles with bedtime doesn't make your problem any easier to solve, but it may make you feel less inadequate, and, therefore, more able to tackle the problem—now.

What's the Rule? is a no-nonsense solution for parents who are ready to make a change for the better in the lives of their children. Please understand that this system is not *easy*, but it is *simple*. We will help you get there!

Hopefully, you will have a few chuckles along the way. After all, if you can't read the book because it is boring, it doesn't matter if we have developed the best technique in the world for getting kids to bed. We have tried, therefore, to make it interesting and fun. It is full of stories of good parents, who are having horrendous problems with bed-time. Brace yourself—we are taking you into real families, and what you'll read isn't always pretty. Of course, some of the stories are funny, because—honestly—a lot of the stuff we get bent out of shape about is pretty silly. Some of the stories are sad, others full of frustration and angst. They are all true, however, and that probably makes this book unique. Although we have changed the names to protect patient con-fidentiality, the people and situations we describe are real. You will absolutely see yourself and your kids in these pages. But, don't worry; we're suckers for happy endings! Read on, good parent, and decide for yourself.

The Technique

Our technique, What's the Rule? has been used by parents in all sorts of situations. It is successful with children as young as 2 years of age and even with teenagers. The posi-tive response of parents and children to this simple way of gaining control of the nighttime routine—going to bed on time, without a fuss, stalling, repeated demands, arguing, or tantrums AND having children sleep in their own beds through the night—is astounding.

Storm Alert

We caution parents, however, against using the word *easy* when describing this method. The truth is that many parents report having three or four absolutely awful nights. That's the bad news. The good news is that, after that, the storm has passed. After the rules are established, change will occur quickly.

The challenge is that the "storm" occurs at night, when parents are tired, cranky, and worn down. This is the time when most of us are the *least* likely to have the stamina and willingness to be consistent. This system requires that you follow it with 100% consistency. But think about it: three or four tough nights in exchange for years of pleasant bedtimes, OR, more months—possibly years—of stressful, unpleasant evenings. Hmm, when you look at it that way, it doesn't seem like a very difficult decision, does it?

The Benefits

Many parents with whom we have worked have found that after following What's the Rule? for a few weeks, not only are the evenings enjoyable for both parents and children but also the children seem to be calmer and better behaved during the day. Other parents report more respectful attitudes and fewer behavior issues with their children. Teachers notice an increase in children's attention and obedience. In all children, we see a dramatic increase in self-esteem.

The basis for this system is setting rules for your household and showing children ways of honoring those rules. This is a system built on consistency. Parents who have tried other methods such as punishment, reward systems, or systems based on social cues have found that, sooner or later, they must still be around to direct the child. What's the Rule? is self-reinforcing and offers a long-term solution. Self-reinforcing means that, after the system is in place, there is no longer any need for the parent to be "the enforcer;" the system runs itself. There will be no need to stay on top of your child by badgering him or reminding her. Unfortunately, other types of systems simply lead to more discussion, which, in turn, leads to arguments.

As we mentioned in the Introduction, there also is a bonus. Once What's the Rule? is in place, you and your child will find it easier to tackle other problems, such as homework completion and first-thing-in-the-morning routines. To borrow a construction analogy, once you have a good framework, the walls are a lot easier to build. This technique provides you and your kids with that framework.

Einstein Was Right!

Some parents keep trying the same failed techniques over and over again. The truth was best summed up by Albert Einstein when he said, "Insanity is doing the same thing over and over again and expecting different results." It's time to admit that THIS JUST ISN'T WORKING!

You are all good parents who have good children. You all deserve to have a simple bedtime routine for your child that results in a good night's sleep for you. Does this seem too good to be true? It isn't. We are going to show you *exactly* how to do it. Bedtime can be pleasant—fun, too!

Conclusion

Bedtime challenges are just that: challenges. Challenges can be overcome, when the most appropriate tools are employed.

We are giving you the tools to deal effectively with the troublesome bedtime behaviors of your kids. Everything you need to know is within these pages. Soon, you will know the "thrill of victory" that comes from triumphing over bedtime challenges.

CHAPTER TWO

Help Is on the Way

W E HOPE YOU are beginning to see a glimmer of light at the end of tunnel and realize that, regardless of your current situation, a stress-free bedtime routine and an uninterrupted night's sleep really are possible. Our goal is to teach you the same simple techniques we have taught thousands of patients.

A Few Parents' Perspectives on Bedtime

Joel and Linda didn't understand why their 7-year-old son David would act like an angel all day at school but the second he got home would be horribly abusive to them. His temper tantrums and demands were out of control. Linda secretly wondered if David had bi-polar disorder but was too embarrassed to bring it up to her husband. She felt like a bad mom for even thinking it.

"Dr. Pressman outlined the system and gave us our marching orders. The first three nights were hell. However, Dr. Pressman had prepared us for an uphill battle. He was familiar with my son's personality. Honestly, we were almost ready to give up until something crazy happened. It worked. It worked exactly the way Dr. Pressman said it would. Oh, and I am no longer concerned that my son has bi-polar disorder."

Jemma read every baby book and parenting book she could get her hands on. As soon as one system failed, she would try another.

"I thought I was doing the right thing by co-sleeping with my daughter. The truth is, I wasn't getting any sleep and my husband and I weren't having sex. By the time we realized maybe this co-sleeping thing wasn't going to work for us, it was just too late. If we switched now, our daughter was going to feel rejected and think we didn't love her...or so we thought. We tried so many different methods of getting our daughter out of our bed; I never imagined that after a few meetings with Stephanie, the problem would be solved. The best part of What's the Rule? is that it makes sense. It's not mean and it's not harsh. I feel like a better parent now, and I definitely feel like I have more adult time with my husband!"

Tom's father was very strict growing up. Bedtime was never an issue in his house, because acting up meant getting spanked.

"My 3-year-old daughter, Julia, would send me through the roof at bedtime. I would think, 'How can something so small be so loud and demanding?' We would put her to bed and she would be up asking for God knows what all night. Finally, we would just give in and bring her in bed with us and hope we got four hours of sleep. I was getting to the point where I felt like maybe what she really needed was a good crack on the butt! My wife made an appointment with Dr. Pressman and he explained the system to us. It seemed to make sense, so we went home and tried it. It took about a week, and each night got a little better. Now if Julia tries to come in bed with us, we just have to look at her and ask, 'What's the rule?' She goes right back in her room."

Moving Ahead

Whether your own situation mirrors one of those above or is entirely different, you have one thing in common with Joel, Linda, Jemma, and Tom: you are not having good nights, and you are ready to try something new. Therefore, once you have finished reading this book, we recommend starting the system as soon as possible. We suggest that you pick up a copy of our companion book, *Matilda and Maxwell's Good Night,* for your child, if you have not already done so. Then talk to your spouse, partner, or other adults in your household and set up a parent meeting to discuss this book and find an appropriate date to begin a new, saner method of parenting: one that lets children learn how to go to bed on time and sleep in their own beds and allows parents to have a pleasant evening—and get a decent night's sleep!

Conclusion

When parents come to our office for an initial consultation and report on the troublesome behaviors of their child, it would be easy for an observer to assume that they are talking about a 400 pound gorilla who has taken up residence in their home. The problem behaviors presented day after day by children can wear down parents' resolve to be fair, loving, sensible, compassionate, and firm. In fact, many parents ruefully describe seeing their child as a "monster" instead of the cute, tiny 4-year-old person who is playing with the puppets in our waiting room. They feel helpless, out of control, and angry—at themselves and at the 400 pound gorilla.

These are not bad parents; these are good parents who need some help. None of us are born knowing good parenting skills, but we can learn them. This book provides a giant forward step in that learning process.

CHAPTER THREE

The "Why" Behind "How You Got Here"

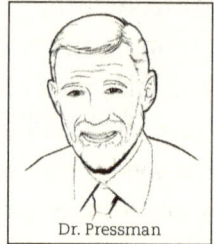

Dr. Pressman

PARENTS OFTEN WORRY that having their children sleep in their own rooms is somehow sending the message to their children that they are rejecting them. Let's look at this idea for a moment to see if it makes sense.

There is a natural and continuous progression of separation between parent and child. Initially, babies are separated from the womb, where they were joined to the mother by the umbilical cord. What is the first thing that is done after the baby is born? This cord is cut. Thus starts the journey away from dependency toward autonomy.

Babies and toddlers eventually have to be separated from the breast or the bottle. Some children even reject these sources on their own. I will never forget the day my daughter Rebecca, at 8 months old, refused to breast-feed from her mother. Stephanie, my wife, had really looked forward to breast-feeding her for the first year. Then one day, out of the blue, Rebecca simply refused to nurse. This is the way so many changes occur with our children. Often emotionally, it is the *parents* who are not ready to cut the psychological cord.

The Mommy's Perspective

Think back to when you were a child. You really had very little that was just yours. Very young children can claim ownership of—well, not much! A special blanket, some dolls or toys, and even those aren't really owned by the child; they can be taken away by a parent. "No, Mommy. That's mine!" is my 2½ year old's frequent assertion.

Mommy Rebecca

As adults, we own houses (and, unfortunately, mortgages), cars, clothes, appliances, this book, etc. One of the very few things to which our child can claim ownership is her *bed*. This is the first and most important place where children learn to take care of themselves psychologically. This is the place where they sleep, calm themselves down, think, and dream. This is the first place where a child learns the pride of taking care of herself. She can sleep alone in her bed, all night long—independent of her parents.

Establishing Identity

Dr. Pressman

Parents often feel that by allowing their child to sleep with them, they are making that child feel more secure. They don't realize that night-time separation, though initially uncomfortable for the child (and often for the parent!), is developmentally *essential*.

In our culture, when this part of a child's development is missing, something very interesting happens. Instead of becoming more *secure* as they grow, they actually become more *insecure*. Think about it. Children learn through a system of trial and error. They try something, it doesn't work, so they try something else; eventually, they find something that works—learning occurs. At every step along the way, the child gains a measure of confidence and feels that he can be a bit more self-sufficient.

Therefore, it's important for parents to provide children with structured opportunities to learn that they can be independent. One of the biggest and best opportunities occurs in a child's own bed. If a child is denied the opportunity to sleep in his own bed, he will not learn to feel secure in the absence of a parent or caregiver.

⚠ Cautionary Note!

Independence leads to autonomy. This is the knowledge that one possesses all the skills he needs to take care of him/herself. Self-confidence of this kind is gained by passing through predictable and necessary stages of separation. When parents do not create the opportunities for children to separate in healthy ways, the children will ultimately *force* separation between themselves and their caregivers in other, perhaps problematic, ways.

The Facts about Separation

This brings us back to the initial concern: will my child think I am rejecting her if I insist that she sleeps in her own bed? The answer is an emphatic, No! In fact, as a child

Stephanie, LICSW

gets older, certainly by the age of 8, the child will attempt to initiate separation in one of two ways:

1. By dramatically misbehaving (hitting or kicking the mother, screaming at her, refusing any commands or requests, or having violent temper tantrums) in an effort to psychologically separate during the daytime. This is due to the extraordinary difficulty in separating during the evening. Joel and Linda's son, David, was one such child. (See Chapter Two, page 15.)

2. By having such profound separation anxiety that the child becomes virtually unable to function in the absence of the mother. For example:

Emma (age 2) would cry inconsolably whenever her mother left her to go to work. She would cry so hard that she would throw up.

Ethan (age 10) would refuse to go to a friend's house unless his mother went with him—and stayed. If he was invited to a birthday party, he insisted that his mother stay at the party. When his mother—becoming embarrassed that she was the only mother staying for the party—insisted on leaving, Ethan would call her repeatedly with complaints ("my stomach hurts," "I fell down," etc.) and demands to be picked up. By the age of 10, he had never attended a sleepover and stayed all night.

Jimmy was the baby of the family. Separated by 12 years from his next oldest sibling, his mother, Ella, didn't want him to "grow up too fast," because he was the last baby she could have. Ella came to see me when Jimmy was 11. The school had told her that she needed to get help for Jimmy, because he was bullying other students and stealing their lunch money and snacks. Ella was distraught; this was her baby, after all. She kept saying what a sweet boy he was but finally disclosed that there had been "some problems at home." Jimmy frequently refused to do what his mother asked, and the arguments had turned into pushing and hitting—from both sides. Good parent that she was, Ella took the blame for the problems, saying that she was tired when she got home from work, so she wasn't very patient.

Parents who either experience unwanted daytime behavior from their child or who hear about it from the school are usually going through two things simultaneously:

1. The child is misbehaving at bedtime—not adhering to an established bedtime routine, not going to bed calmly, and not staying in her room all night.

2. The good parent is involved in making up excuses for the child's problem behavior (e.g., justifying the child's nocturnal activities, minimizing and/or blaming someone else like him- or herself, a spouse, or the teacher) for the child's daytime problems.

When no one in the house is sleeping well, it's hard to keep up the pretence of "all's well; we've just hit a little bump in the road." The parents are tired, and the children are uncooperative, insecure, and needy; nobody's having fun, but everybody's afraid to change—things might get worse! In *none* of the four previous examples did parents seek counseling because of bedtime problems. They never even considered the possibility that bedtime behavior was related to daytime issues, yet David, Emma, Ethan, and Jimmy were all sleeping in the parents' bed. For example, Dr. Pressman ultimately discovered from Jimmy's mother, Ella, that Jimmy had started sleeping in his mother's bed when he was 18 months old—the night after his father walked out on them. With embarrassment, Ella explained that Jimmy still climbed in bed with her after she fell asleep; she didn't have the heart to kick him out.

You will meet these children again. In every case, when What's the Rule? was used to settle the bedtime issues, the problem behaviors quickly resolved. Coincidence? We don't think so; you decide.

A Pattern Emerges

After 35 years of treating children and their families, I recognized a definite pattern. Pediatric patients came in with a variety

Dr. Pressman

of symptoms, described by their parents as ranging from hyperactivity to depression to bad behavior. When calling for the initial appointment, a mother usually cites problems in school, defiance at home, tantrums, separation anxiety, or some other problem behavior of her child as the reason for calling. No parent ever made an appointment because her child was having bedtime problems.

At first glance, these cases appear to have little in common. The symptoms and problems differ from family to family. However, I invariably find that all of these cases have one thing in common: the children are not always sleeping in their own beds. The impact and strain of this behavior on the family is so powerful that I now ask all new patients during the first session where family members routinely sleep. Invariably, the child about whom the appointment was made is

1. not going to bed at a regular time, and

2. is not staying in her room all night.

Most parents know, in their hearts, that it is probably better to have their child sleeping peacefully in his *own* bed. But, in spite of the stresses—unpleasant evenings and parental interrupted sleep—parents are not able to connect problem behaviors at bedtime with behavioral problems during the day. The root cause of many behavior problems in children is related to chaotic bedtimes.

In the case of Ella's son, Jimmy, the cause of his acting out was obvious; he was forcing a separation from his mother during the daytime that he was unable to do at night. With the help of both individual and micro-group therapy[1] for Ella and Jimmy, What's the Rule? was started. Jimmy and Ella

---

[1] Developed by Dr. Robert Pressman, dual micro-group psychotherapy consists of both a parent's and a child's group, each containing three patients, which meet at the same time. The parent group has one therapist; the child group has one therapist and an assistant.

gained confidence in their ability to be apart at night and to act as a team in the daytime.

The Mommy's Perspective ⇨ on Why

Think about it. It's not as if your child was born at the age of 2 or 3. She starts out as this adorable little bit of a thing. You may find that you get up at night to change her diaper and bring her back into bed with you so that she can get fed and cuddled. It's a wonderful bonding time and you often find that you don't even have to wake up all the way to do it.

Mommy Rebecca

Then she's a little older and she can't fall asleep, or she gets the flu or a really bad cold or croup and you bring her into bed so you can doze and keep an eye on her at the same time. It's comforting to have her in bed with you; she's so cute and cuddly and it's a great excuse just to hold her, smell her baby hair, and know that you're keeping her safe. Of course, you don't really sleep—you can't.

Then, suddenly she's 6 or 8, and she throws tantrums at bedtime or watches the 11 o'clock news with you and usually ends up in your bed and you are TIRED: tired of and tired from nightly struggles and lack of sleep. She's in your bed more than her own anyway, so why go through all the hassle and arguing when you know how it's going to end? Even if you knew what to do, you're too tired to do it.

Conclusion

You have only met a few parents and children so far. Yet, even this small sampling gives you a good idea of the importance of the bedtime routine. We have outlined the reasons why children need to separate from their parents, both psychologically and physically. As a parent, we control some important aspects of how and when it happens. A reasonable and consistent bedtime routine is a critical piece of the healthy separation process.

There will be many more real stories throughout the book. And, don't forget, there's also a book for your children: *Matilda and Maxwell's Good Night.* Your kids will love it, and so will you; it's very funny. So, let's move on to Part Two: "What's the Rule? Everything You Want to Know!"

WHAT'S the RULE?
Everything You WANT TO KNOW!

CHAPTER FOUR

Rules vs. Commands

Commands

A *command* is an order or a demand; it is a directive given to cause action. Commands are given by people who are "in charge" of other people, and they imply authority, domination, and control.

Stephanie, LICSW

Unless you are working within an authoritarian structure, like the military, you probably don't like to be ordered to do something. It is not surprising, therefore, that when we use commands with children, we tend to get resistance. The problem with commands is that the only correct answer a child can give is "yes."

Even a request from a parent can feel like a command to a child, especially if it is unexpected or if the child is involved in an activity. The polite, "Please go wash your hands for dinner," will be reacted to as if it had been delivered, "Go wash, now!" if the child is in the middle of an episode of Sesame Street or SpongeBob Squarepants.

Because children—just like adults—don't like to feel they are being ordered around, they usually don't respond with the "correct" answer. When children don't respond appropriately to a command, parents then have to deal with the child's *inappropriate* response. You many not realize it, but all of the following are forms of commands:

1. Please clean your room.

2. Let's eat dinner before we watch TV, OK?

3. Don't you think you should do your homework?

Unless the child (1) says "Yes" and runs to her room, (2) immediately turns off the TV, or (3) grabs her books from her backpack, a problem has been created.

Commands Create Problems

Commands create problems, for both kids and parents. Parents feel like "nags" or "the hygiene police" or "the homework Nazi"—all direct quotes from my patients. Good parents don't want to constantly remind their good children to do things—day after day after day.

Following are more direct quotes from the good parents we see every day. When you read them, they're pretty funny. When you *live* them, they're pretty frustrating.

- ◆ **"Brush your teeth."** "Did you brush your teeth?" "Go brush your teeth!"

- ◆ **"Every damn night** I have to remind him to put his completed homework into his backpack— every damn night!"

- ◆ **"Do you think** she could remember to go to the bathroom before she gets into bed? No! Every night I have to tell her, 'Go to the potty before we go upstairs.' Jeez!"

- ◆ **"She has to** put on pajamas every night. But, every night, it's, like, 'Pajamas? I have to put on pajamas?'—like it's some big surprise! Can 3 year olds get Alzheimer's?"

Commands are orders; they may be inconsistent, unpredictable and often erratic. Even if the same commands are issued on a regular basis, e.g., "Brush your teeth!" said nightly, they almost always feel unfair to the person receiving them. Commands are not mutually rewarding—parents rarely enjoy giving them, and children rarely enjoy receiving them. Commands lead to dissention and resentment.

Rules

A *rule* is a guide for conduct and actions. It is an accepted procedure that leads to a habit.

After a rule is established, there is no need for reminding or nagging and the resultant frustration and anger. Rules lead to consistency, regularity, predictability, security, and safety. The child knows what to expect, can predict the course of events, and gains a sense of safety from the routine. A good rule is useful, mutually rewarding, and results in relaxed, focused activity.

The biggest problem good parents have with their children's bedtime is that it degenerates into a series of commands—Take your bath! Brush your teeth! No more TV! You don't need a snack! No more stories!

It's exhausting to reinforce commands and they are never self-reinforcing. You will always have to be there to make sure it happens, and you will always have to be there to punish your child when one of two things happen:

1. He doesn't do it.

2. He responds with any answer other than "yes."

The best part about the What's the Rule? technique is that once it is established, it is self-reinforcing.

The Mommy's Perspective

When I was growing up, my mother had a rule that we had to take off our shoes before coming in the house. We would leave them in the entryway. To this day, I still take my shoes off when entering not only my house but also other

Mommy Rebecca

people's houses. This rule is so engrained that I established it for my own family as soon as I was married. Now that I have two kids, they also follow the rule.

The first thing my 2-year-old daughter does after coming in the house is to remove her shoes. If she has any difficulty in getting them off, she immediately yells, "Shoes off! Hunter needs shoes off!" It's very cute.

Of course, it is also interesting when someone new comes in the house, and Hunter immediately instructs them, "Shoes off! Take shoes off!" They always do. (The UPS man knows to NEVER step inside; he wears lace-up boots.)

Hunter's bedtime routine is followed with the same attention to the rules. If I try to read just two books instead of three or if I sing the bedtime songs out of order, Hunter will correct me every time.

Because 100% consistency is necessary when using this system, rules should be thought of as permanent. You want to be careful, therefore, to make rules only concerning issues or events that have real value to your family. Bedtime is an important event in every family. Obviously, having a clean floor was an important issue for my mother and is now a habit for me. Different strokes…

An Annual Event…Perhaps

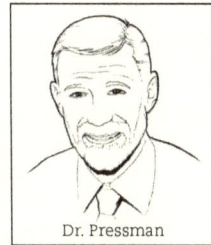
Dr. Pressman

A possible exception to the permanency-of-rules condition is that, as your child gets older, his bedtime may switch from, say, 7:00 to 8:00 P.M. The spirit of the rule is the same; the time is merely altered. However, changing a rule will be incredibly rare. That's why, when making a rule, you will want to first run it through what we like to call the rule filter, which is explained in Chapter Five.

Conclusion

It's easy to spot homes where commands are used a lot. There is way too much talking—and noise! Children will argue, plead, rationalize, negotiate, and stage dramatic scenes that put William Shakespeare to shame. Parents will repeat, justify, promise, threaten, nag, remind, and yell—until everyone ultimately feels upset and disrespected.

Rules are sane, positive, and respectful. They don't require constant vigilance on the part of the parents or engender hurt or angry feelings in the children. Rules are way cooler—if you learn how to effectively design them.

CHAPTER FIVE

The Rule Filter

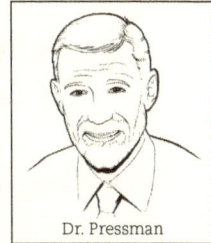

Dr. Pressman

NOW THAT YOU UNDERSTAND the difference between a rule and a command, it's important to make certain a rule is going to work. We recommend using the rule filter before announcing a new rule. This filter is a surefire way of catching problems that can occur with a new rule.

In order to work, rules need to be

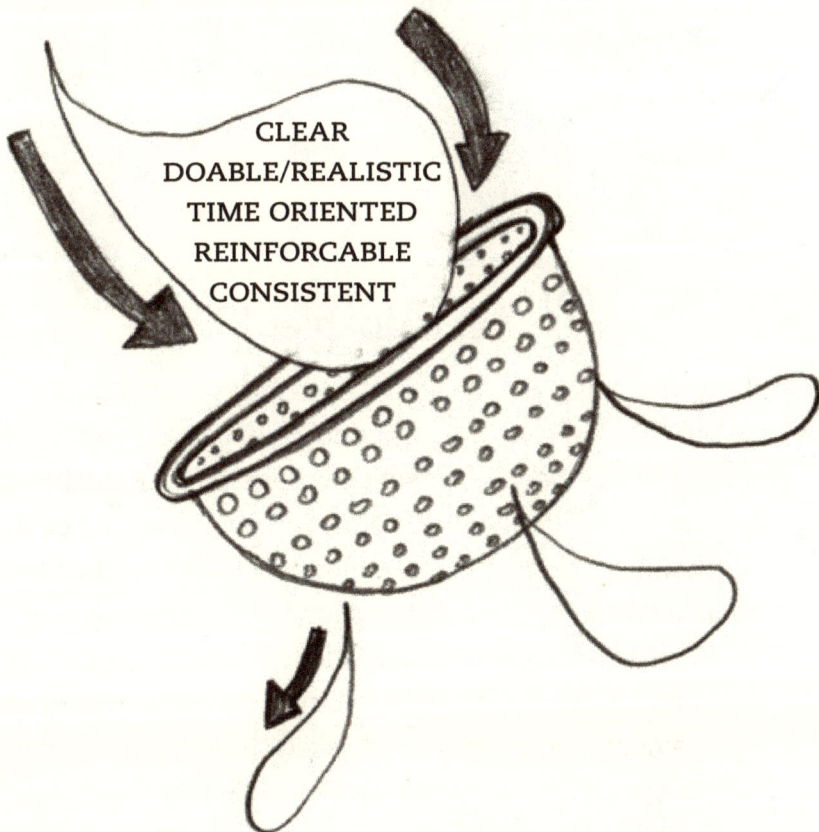

CLEAR
DOABLE/REALISTIC
TIME ORIENTED
REINFORCABLE
CONSISTENT

❓ "Is it clear?" ❓

Let's take a moment to examine each of these steps in establishing a rule. The first step in the filter is that the rule must be clear. Telling a child "bedtime is *between* 7:30 and 8:00" is not clear. Telling a child "bedtime means in your own bed *at* 8:00 P.M." is clear.

Which rules are clear? Choose A or B.

A. Clean your room on Saturday.

B. Put all your clothes in the hamper before dinner.

Or another one: Choose C or D.

C. No TV after dinner.

D. Don't watch violent movies.

You chose B and C, correct? See, this is simple stuff—so far.

❓ "Is it doable?" ❓

I like to use this extreme, laughable example. You tell your 6 year old that he will change the oil of your car every Friday morning before he goes to school. Clear, but not doable. On the other hand, being in bed at 7:30 is both clear and doable.

Sometimes rules *seem* both clear and doable—but there may be a problem. Look at the following example of a child's bedtime that was not set at a realistic time.

Joel and Linda couldn't understand why they were unable to get David in bed by 7:00 P.M. I asked these parents to write down the activities they performed with David before bed and give a guesstimate for the time it took to complete each one. Working backwards, look at the timetable Joel and Linda described:

- Put in bed—1 minute

- Singing the special bedtime song—3 minutes

- Reading three stories—10 minutes

- Brushing teeth and using toilet—5 minutes

- Watching a special video and having a snack—20 minutes

- Taking a bath, drying, dressing in pajamas—20 minutes

As they were surprised to discover, the pre-bedtime activities took an hour. Because their dinnertime was seldom finished before 6:30, the 7:00 bedtime was unrealistic. Based on the second step in the filter, they realized that they needed to change his bedtime to 7:45. Now, there are no problems.

Which are doable/realistic rules—choose A or B.
Which one is within your child's ability to carry out?

A. Do not go to the bathroom until the morning.

B. Go to the bathroom at night (if you must), but return to your bed immediately.

Again, which is the more realistic rule—C or D?
Which one is specific and reasonable?
Getting trickier, aren't we?

C. Be ready for school before the bus comes.

D. Pack your backpack before shower time.

Answers B and D are both realistic and reasonable.

❓ "Is it time-oriented?" ❓

Children—although they will never admit it—crave schedules and consistency. Therefore, when deciding on a going-to-bed rule for your family, make sure that your child absolutely understands when bedtime is to occur.

There are three ways that time can be expressed. The most obvious is the exact time (i.e., 8:30 P.M.). This is the best way to set bedtimes. For other types of rules, the time may be set before an event (i.e., before dinner) or after an event (i.e., after school). Some rules, such as sleepovers, have beginnings and endings (e.g., from 5:00 P.M. to 11:00 A.M.).

As parents, having a realistic time orientation makes our lives much simpler. Make sure that when communicating with your child, you are time-oriented.

> *In terms of time orientation, will choice A or choice B be easier for a child to accomplish? Which one gives a clear time frame for your child to understand?*
>
> A. Get your stuff out of the family room on Saturday.
> B. Have your sneakers and backpack in your room before dinner.
>
> Yes, the correct answer is B.

❓ "Is it reinforceable?" ❓

One of the best parts of this system is that once a rule is well-established, it becomes self-reinforcing. However, in the beginning, it is essential that parents or caregivers are present and on the same page in terms of understanding and agreeing to the rules in order to reinforce them. If the mother and father live in the same house and the mother reinforces the rule but the father does not, then the rule is not consistently reinforceable.

Which rule can you be there to check and support?

A. Brush your teeth at school after lunch.

B. Brush your teeth before you go to school.

Aha! Of course, you said B. You're getting better at this.

The Reinforcement Riddle

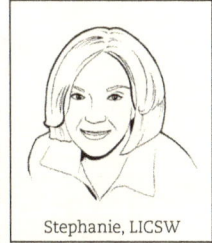

Stephanie, LICSW

For a child, getting attention from a parent is a powerful reinforcement. When you set up the new bedtime rules, make sure they are simple and clear, so they are easily reinforced. If there have been problems at bedtime, then *problem behaviors* have been getting attention—and have been reinforced. For example, if a child cries and whines and then is yelled at, he's getting attention—the problem behavior is being reinforced. If a child kicks and screams and then gets picked up and carried to her room by an adult, then she's getting attention and physical contact—the problem behavior is being reinforced.

When we get to Chapter Six, we'll talk more about this. For now, just remember to give attention ONLY to the behaviors you wish to be learned and repeated, and make sure that you are there to actually give the attention—every time during the first two weeks.

"Will it remain consistent?"

Consistency and reinforcement are strongly tied together. It is essential that rules are *always* reinforced. If you are not able to be physically present to reinforce the new rule, it will be NOT be consistently reinforced. Without absolute consistency, the system will not work.

The issue of consistency is a significant factor in deciding when to introduce the rule. If you know that you are going on vacation next week or that one of the children is going to Grandma's for three days, you will not be able to reinforce the rule consistently. You need to set aside the time necessary (two weeks, to be on the safe side) to know that you and your children will be at home to make sure the rule is firmly established.

If, as parents, we are not consistent with our rules, then we are quite literally teaching our child that rules are made to be broken. Your child is smart! If she can get you to forget the rule, she will—and then it will be much more difficult to establish the rule the next time. Therefore, while you are establishing What's the Rule? at bedtime, you can't have another caregiver put the kids to bed; you can't make exceptions (like when Uncle Jake comes to visit) or use excuses (Daddy's been gone all week—we'll let the kids stay up *just this once*). *After* the rule is firmly established, then exceptions will occur—usually with planning and preparation—but not during the first few weeks.

You're almost through—hang tough! This one is harsh! Choose A or B.

During the first week of the new bedtime routine, Dad is offered tickets to an all-star game.

A. Mom and Dad recognize that this is a wonderful opportunity, so they decide to go. However, they give the sitter—Auntie Marilyn—**very specific instructions** about the bedtime routine.

B. Mom and Dad recognize that this is a wonderful opportunity, so it is very hard to turn down. They decide that there will be other games, but this is their best shot at getting the bedtime routine well established with Junior. They've already put in two nights of misery; they're certainly not going to throw it all away now. They made a commitment to each other to stay home with Junior for two weeks, so they regretfully decline the tickets. Tonight could be the night that cements the new routine!

Did you choose B? Of course you did. It hurt, though, didn't it? But you need to keep the big picture in mind: Endless nights of calm bedtimes, hours of unbroken sleep—unless your mate snores, and we can't help you with that.

Conclusion

Thoughtful rules, carefully designed and consistently supported, are the underpinnings of a smoothly run home. When rules can be twisted, negotiated, pleaded, or promised away by the children, dissatisfaction and behavioral acting out will follow. The children in this situation have too much power; they sense it, so they must continually test it until a boundary is set. Boundaries or rules may not be greeted with joy by the children, but they give a sense of safety, which children crave. Of course, the new boundaries will be tested to see if they are real.

When rules are ignored, forgotten ("Oh, my! It can't be 10:30 already!"), altered, or suspended for the convenience of the parents, guess what happens? Dissatisfaction and behavioral acting out by the children will follow! New, often unrealistic and ill-considered rules may then be hastily announced to "punish" the children for their ingratitude and "taking advantage" of the generosity of the parent.

The obvious lesson is as follows: Have a few carefully chosen rules, consistently reinforced, and starting with bedtime. Habits will be formed that go a long way to making your home a calmer, happier place for everyone. So, are you ready? Here comes the description of the four-step process that will lead you to your families' best bedtime routine—ever!

CHAPTER SIX

The Four-Step Process of Establishing "What's the Rule?"

Framing
the Rule

THE FIRST STEP in the process involves deciding what the rule is going to be. Obviously, establishing rules can work for a variety of problems in your home and can extend beyond the issue of bedtime. However, remember the five rule filters covered in Chapter Five. Rules must be doable and reinforceable. Bombarding your kids with a new list of rules is going to be overwhelming for them and impossible for you to reinforce. I recommend tackling bedtime for

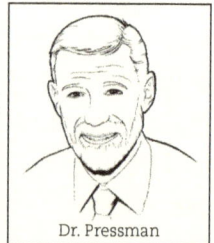

Dr. Pressman

now and waiting until that system is self-reinforcing before moving on to any other behavioral issues.

When framing the new rule, I recommend that parents and caregivers have a meeting to decide what the bedtime rule will be. It is important that all caregivers who live in the house with the child are in agreement regarding the rule. The bedtime rule will be different in every house depending on a variety of factors. The critical thing is that it passes the five guidelines for filtering rules.

Now we are going to introduce you to Julia and Rick and their son, R.J., and follow them through the four-step process of establishing the rule.

Julia and Rick's Story

Julia and Rick are a professional couple in their mid-30s. Julia started her own marketing and public relations firm five years ago and has been extremely successful. Her husband, Rick, is "a financial genius," according to Julia. "I don't have a clue what he does, but evidently he does it very well."

Six years ago, they purchased an apartment in a large city. Centrally located, with a decent size bedroom and even a small dining room, the apartment was perfect for the busy couple. When Julia became pregnant, they put up a wall in the dining room and created a small nursery.

Both Rick and Julia's jobs called for them to have business-related social functions during evening hours. Some of Julia's jobs, for example, being on the set of commercials or with clients for television tapings, called for her to work very late. Fortunately, a family with two teenage daughters lived in the same building, and both girls were enthusiastic and experienced babysitters.

R.J., as their baby was immediately nicknamed, was a high energy child. Many parents would have wondered if he had ADHD (Attention Deficit Hyperactive Disorder) almost from birth, but both Julia and Rick were active adults, so they loved R.J.'s energy and activity.

When he was an infant, Julia often took R.J. with her to work. The setting up of photo shoots and other kinds of publicity arrangements were usually busy, informal affairs that occurred outside; the presence of an infant was not a problem. When R.J. became a busy toddler, babysitters had to be used increasingly.

Seemingly overnight, R.J. turned from being an adorable, curious live-wire, to a demanding, tantrum-throwing, unhappy little 4 year old. When his preschool teacher suggested that they might want to consult with a child psychologist about the changes in R.J.'s behavior, Julia and Rick came in for counseling.

Rick: R.J. seems so angry all the time. Just yesterday, we were in the hardware store in our neighborhood. R.J. loves to go there. We just hang out; the old guy who owns it likes kids, so he usually has a treat for R.J. Anyway, for no reason at all, R.J. just takes a handful of screws and throws them. Then, he lies down and starts kicking and screaming. I mean—there was no reason! I don't get it. We've really tried to adjust our schedules so that one of us is usually with him—we know he was starting to be with babysitters too much. I mean, they're good baby-sitters, but they're not his parents.

Julia: I feel like it's my fault. I honestly thought that taking him with me to work was good for him. He seemed happy and entertained. But he's gotten so demanding...I don't know...nothing I do seems right any more. Maybe I should just quit work.

Rick: It's not Julia's fault. She's a great mother. I wish she'd been MY mother—if you know what I mean.

Julia: [smiling] That sounds a little weird, Rick.

Rick: Right. Anyway, it's just that she's so creative. She really plays with him a lot; she takes him to parks and museums and all over. He has play groups they go to. But now his school says he's hitting; he throws a fit if he has to share. After yesterday, I believe them. That was a bad scene.

Julia: His teacher is such a sweetie; I really felt embarrassed when she called us in. She pretty much said that R.J. has some serious behavioral issues. My baby boy.... [Julia starts to cry]

Let's Talk about Bedtime

At this point in the interview, I typically cover family history, the mother's pregnancy, the child's developmental milestones, and other relevant historical, medical, and psychological data. Then, I ask about sleeping arrangements.

Dr. Pressman: Tell me about R.J.'s bedtime routine. Does he sleep in his own bed?

[Julia and Rick look embarrassed. Julia twists her sweater.]

Rick: This is kind of a sore spot for us. My mother-in-law's been on our case for months.

Because of his parent's irregular and often unpredictable schedules, as an infant R.J. would often just fall asleep in his snuggy or carriage—wherever Julia might be. As he got older, he was allowed to stay up later than usual, so he could spend time with one parent or the other. When Rick had to travel, he would sometimes awaken R.J. late at night to be able to play and cuddle with him.

This erratic schedule did not lend itself to the establishment of a calm bedtime routine. Rather, R.J. was trained to be up with a parent at the time most children are in their bed, alone.

When Julia would try to institute a bedtime routine, either outside circumstances or R.J. himself would sabotage it. The result was that R.J. ended up in his parents' bed virtually every night.

Framing the Rule. Continued

Once Julia and Rick understood the role that bedtime plays in the establishment of children's autonomy, behavior, and healthy development, they were ready to consider trying the What's the Rule? technique. They had been truly disturbed by the teacher's report, and, as good parents, wanted to do whatever they could to help R.J. through this difficult time. They also thought that being able to sleep through the night would be a worthwhile bonus!

They set 7:00 P.M. as a reasonable bedtime and pledged to have at least one parent home by 5:00 for the next month. Because R.J. had no planned activities that ended after 4:00, his schedule was not a problem.

The Rule: R.J. will be in his own bed for the night by 7:00 P.M.

Clear: Yes
Doable/Realistic: Yes

Given the decision reached by both parents, a 7:00 P.M. bedtime seemed both **Clear** and **Doable/Reasonable**.

2

Deciding When to Implement the Rule

Once the rule has been fully defined and all caregivers are on the same page, it is time to determine when to implement it. For any rule to meet the criteria set forth in the rule filter, it must be consistent and reinforceable. This is why deciding *when* to implement the rule is extremely important. As mentioned earlier, the best part about this system is that, in time, it will become self-reinforcing. In the beginning, however, you will need to reinforce the rule and be consistent in doing so. Parents should minimally commit to two weeks of total structure of the bedtime routine while the rule is being established.

Therefore, I recommend looking at your schedules and choosing a time in your lives when you can realistically dedicate a couple of weeks to staying at home with your children during bedtime. The week before a planned vacation is not the time to start a new routine requiring a new rule.

However, I caution parents against waiting for "the perfect opportunity," as that time may never come. Resolve to make time in your schedule to start What's the Rule? as soon as possible. Parents who say, "Let's start when school starts" or "We'll start as soon as we have finished redecorating their room," quickly find that these seemingly perfect opportunities are actually just ways to procrastinate. Let's see how Rick and Julia handled the second step in the process.

📖 Julia and Rick's Story Continued

By the next session, both parents had consulted their calendars and decided on a date to start using What's the Rule?

Julia: My parents are coming for three days, so this week won't work.

Rick: Also, my boss has a box for the basketball games, and this weekend is Julia's and my "command performance" attendance.

They decided that they would discuss the new bedtime routine with R.J. the next Sunday morning and would implement it that night. They planned a low-key family day with some outdoors activities. An early pizza dinner would please all of them and would be easy for Julia.

Because at least one parent had committed to be home by 5:00 each night (and, in reality, Rick had a late meeting only once in the first two weeks, and Julia set her own schedule), that meant the rule could be consistently reinforced.

So, let's put it through the rule filter:

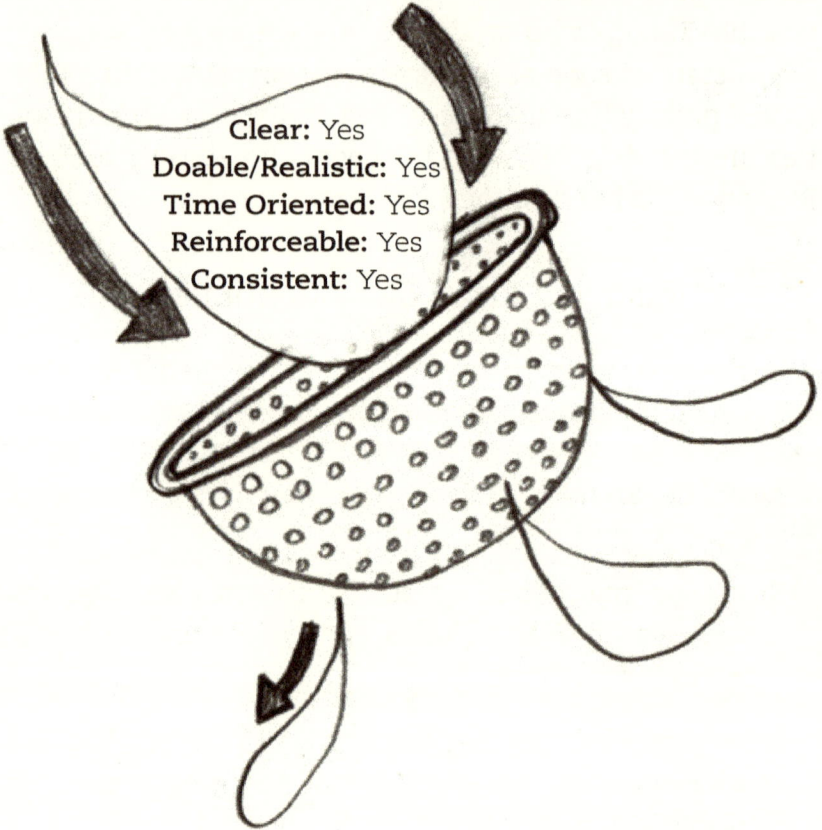

Clear: Yes
Doable/Realistic: Yes
Time Oriented: Yes
Reinforceable: Yes
Consistent: Yes

The new rule passed with flying colors. Julia and Rick were then able to move on to the third step and establish their own unique and specially designed bedtime routine.

3

Establishing
a Bedtime Routine

Children crave consistency. Providing a bedtime routine is a wonderful means of giving them a consistent and pleasant way to wind down and prepare for sleep. The bedtime routine is different in every household, depending on the activities and preferences of both children and parents.

Some children are content to be read to; others prefer to watch a video or sing songs. There are some who like to stay in the tub until they resemble prunes, while, for others, a five minute shower is about three minutes too long. There is really only one consideration when establishing a bedtime routine: events should go from more active to less active.

The Mommy's Perspective

The bedtime routine in our house has always been the same: tubby time, brushing teeth, books, rocking in the rocking chair, and bed. One night, for no particular reason, my daughter, Hunter, ran up the stairs at bedtime and said in her most adorable little voice, "Oh Daddy, I bet you can't catch me!" What ensued was a hilarious chase up the stairs followed by five minutes of tickling on the bed. We were all laughing and it felt great to see my husband and my daughter having a special moment.

However, when we pulled out the books to read, she started jumping on the bed. It took twenty extra minutes to get her to bed. The next night, after Hunter brushed her teeth, she asked for Daddy to chase and tickle her. He was flattered that she wanted his attention (bedtime had become a strictly "mommy routine") and he obliged immediately. The scene from the previous night replayed, except it took 30 extra minutes to get her calm, and she woke up crying once during the night.

New routines and patterns form quickly. They usually emerge from the best of intentions. My daughter and my husband were playing and bonding and I didn't want to get in the way of that. However, it was disrupting the bedtime routine. "Chase and tickle time" now comes directly after dinner—before tubby time and long before bedtime.

Remember…more active to less active!

My oldest daughter, Sarah, was extremely easy to put to bed at night. Her routine consisted of a warm bath, a few books and bed. My son, on the other hand, seemed to require about an hour of wind-down activities before he was ready for bed. His personality was simply different from that of my daughter's—and so were his needs.

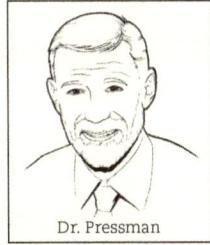

Dr. Pressman

We found that, for him, a 20-minute video followed by coloring was necessary before the bath and books. Although his bedtime was the same as his sister's, his bedtime routine actually started 45 minutes earlier.

Bedtime routines often include one or more of the following elements: television, videos, music, bath/showering, drawing/coloring, brushing teeth, getting on pajamas, reading, singing, saying prayers, etc. Remember to organize the events so that they go from more active to less active. Rick and Julia put a lot of thought into planning a bedtime routine for their son. They were quite creative, as you will see.

Julia and Rick's Story Continued

Rick and Julia came from very different backgrounds. Rick came from a large, working class family, and the children were pretty much on their own. He had no memory of any bedtime routine; he went to bed when his brother did, and usually read under the covers with a flashlight until he fell asleep.

Julia's family was, as she put it, "comfortable." Money was not a problem, her mother stayed home to care for Julia—an only child—and life was full of pleasant routines and rituals.

Julia: I had a great childhood. I really want R.J. to grow up with the same feelings of safety and tradition that I did. It makes me sad to think how out of touch with that I've been. I mean—we do have our own little traditions, don't get me wrong. They just aren't very consistent—especially around bedtime.

The routine that they came up with looked like this:

5:15—5:30 Hall running
5:30—6:00 Dinner
6:00—6:20 Bath, brush teeth, pj's
6:20—6:40 Video
6:40—7:00 Three stories, songs, prayers, bed

You're probably thinking, "Hall running?" Julia and Rick's apartment is on the same floor as two other families with preschoolers. Because they live in the city, and "running around in the yard" isn't a late day option, Julia organized a 15-minute period at the end of the day when R.J. and the two other kids ran up and down the hall to "blow off steam." The other moms loved the idea, and it gave them a social time together. Julia had slipped a note under the doors of the other three tenants, explaining that there would be running sounds in the hall from 5:15 to 5:30 P.M. daily; the other tenants either didn't mind or weren't home, so there were no complaints. Creative, isn't it?

The bedtime routine that Julia and Rick designed was uniquely suited to apartment living in a city with an active 4 year old. You may live on an acre of land in the suburbs or in a Victorian house on a postcard size lot in a town; you may have one child or several. The bedtime routine that you build will be based on the special conditions of your living situation and the special interests and habits of you and your child. That's one of the reasons why it will work.

4

Starting a New Rule

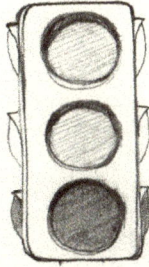

The last step in the process is to introduce the rule to your child, and go over the bedtime routine. We recommend that all caregivers in the house sit down with the child some time substantially before bedtime to discuss it. Morning or early afternoon works best for family meetings.

When introducing rules, we like to use the "How old are you now?" technique. It goes essentially like this. The parent asks the child, "How old are you now?" The child answers, "I am 8." The parent then responds, "Oh, my goodness, you're 8 year's old already? Wow, you're so much older than you used to be! Now that you are so much older, there is a new responsibility that I think you can handle."

This is the time when parents introduce the new rule and cover the bedtime routine. Let's see how Julia and Rick did it with R.J.

Julia and Rick's Story Continued

On Sunday morning, the family was enjoying a special breakfast: pancakes and bacon. As he finished his last bite of bacon, Rick looked at R.J., who was making designs with syrup on his plate.

Rick: R.J., how old are you now?

R.J.: Daddy! You know how old I am! I'm 4!

Rick: [turns to Julia, who is at the sink] Julia, did you know that R.J. is 4 YEARS OLD NOW?

Julia: I'm stunned. You're 4 already?

[R.J. laughs]

Rick: Wow! You're so much older than you used to be! You know, R.J., [Rick now speaks in a serious tone of voice] now that you're so much older, there is a new responsibility that we think you can handle."

R.J.: What's a re—

Rick: A responsibility is like a job. I have a job, Mommy has a job—jobs—and now you'll have one, too.

[R.J. nods his head expectantly]

Rick: Your job—because you're so much older, is that you're going to go to sleep in your own bed, all night long.

[Julia joins them at the table]

Julia: We know that bedtimes have been kind of mixed up. They haven't been very much fun for any of us. So, we're going to set up bedtime as a very special time of day—maybe the best time of day! We're going to have hall running with Kayla and Joachim—every day.

R.J.: [excited] Really? Every day?

Julia: Yup; every day that they're home, they'll be running in the hall with you. If they're away, we'll just run by ourselves.

R.J.: Yippee!

Julia: Then we'll have bath time with some cool new boats—or a shower, if Dad's home. And then we can watch one of your videos. We'll have plenty of time to read you three of your books, and sing some songs before we tuck you in at 7:00. So the new rule is, In bed for the night by 7:00.

Rick: You're getting to be such a big boy, champ. I know you can do this.

Julia: So, big boy, What's the rule?

R.J.: Um—tell me again.

Rick: In bed by 7:00 for the whole night.

R.J.: In bed at 7:00 for the night. All night?

Julia and Rick: All night.

R.J.: But what if I have to pee real bad?

Rick: Then you just get up, go to the bathroom, and go right back to bed.

R.J.: Okay.

Julia: Nice job, R.J.! How about you guys grab our jackets and we go to the park?

Julia and Rick did a terrific job of explaining the rule. They did it in the morning—good job!—as everyone is fresher and more optimistic early in the day. They kept the conversation upbeat and happy. Julia also acknowledged that things had been "kind of mixed up" at night, which R.J. obviously knew. (Stating the obvious—without making a big deal of it—builds credibility with children.) They covered the new bedtime routine and had R.J. repeat the rule. Excellent job, parents!

Reinforcing The Rule: Talking Is Your Worst Enemy!

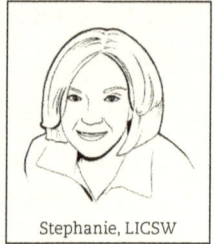

Stephanie, LICSW

Now that the bedtime rule is in place, the time has come to reinforce it. Acceptance of the bedtime rule varies from child to child, depending on her personality. However, most children will test the rule for the first few nights. The key to success is to limit conversation and remain consistent.

A Question, Not a Command

Also, remember that What's the rule? is a question, not a command. The child will either respond with some version of the rule, which you reward with a little smile or head nod, and then you gesture toward the child's room. Or, the child may shrug, indicating she doesn't know, or she may say, "I don't know." You then restate the rule and gesture (open palm—pointing a finger is a command) toward the child's room. Period. Engaging a child in conversation will only serve to stimulate them and aggravate you. I cannot stress this point enough.

Getting Out of Bed and Leaving the Room

Here is how to handle a child getting out of bed. The first time a child gets out of bed and exits her room, ask "What's the rule?" If she does not respond or if she answers with anything other than the rule, simply state the rule. "The rule is in bed for the night at 7:00." Gesture toward the bedroom (palm up, pleasant expression on the face).

The second time the child does it, again ask, "What's the rule?" If the child does not respond correctly—saying the rule and going back to bed—restate the rule and gesture toward the bedroom (palm up, pleasant expression on the face). Also, move toward the bedroom so the action conveys to the child "Come with me" not "Go away!" The action includes the child rather than excluding (rejecting) her. If the child correctly says the rule, then nod, smile, and gesture toward the bedroom.

Every time the child comes out, ask the question "What's the rule?"; the correct answer is restated (if necessary), and non-verbal cues are given (e.g., a nod toward the bedroom, gesturing toward the bedroom, moving near the child's room and beckoning her). It is important not to deviate, elaborate, or add on to the statement of What's the rule?

This is subtle stuff, but kids are experts on reading our body language. That's why I'm trying to paint a picture of what you will look like while you are reinforcing the rule. There can't be anything punitive or angry or irritated about asking "What's the rule?" There is no suggestion of the child being "sent to her room" or banished there; she is going to her room with her parent showing her the way—because that's where she will be comfortable and safe during the night.

Remember the formula: first, simply ask "What's the rule?" If appropriate, restate it. From then on, let your body do the talking. (Make sure it's talking nicely!)

One Last Thing: Beware the Red Herring!

Red herring is a term to describe something that lures you away from the path you want to follow. There are lots of stories about the origin of this term. One is that farmers, tired of having fox hunters trot over their fields, laid out smelly salted herrings to distract the hounds. For our purposes, the red herrings are words or behaviors that your child uses to distract you from following through with What's the Rule?

These are often behaviors for which the child might, under ordinary circumstances, be reprimanded or punished. Following are a few of the classic red herrings dangled by good children in front of good parents during the early phase of establishing the new rule.

◆ Swearing

◆ Kicking or hitting

◆ Throwing a tantrum

◆ Throwing an object

◆ Breaking something

◆ Hysterical crying

◆ Pathetic weeping

◆ Name calling ("Bad Mommy!" "Stupid Daddy!") and "I hate you!"

◆ Development of an ailment

◆ Entering a room with a closed door, without knocking or being given permission to enter—usually the parents' bedroom

◆ Vomiting—I kid you not!

◆ "You don't love me anymore" or "You love [insert sibling's (or pet's) name] more than me!"

It is our job to help you learn not to be distracted by any red herrings your child may offer while you are trying to follow the path to the new bedtime routine.

There will be a time and place to deal with any unwanted behaviors that arise while trying to institute What's the Rule? However, if you chase down every distraction your child throws at you while it is happening, then you fall victim to the red herring trap. A calm parent is also one who is not easily distracted and is able to keep her eye on the prize! NOTHING is more important during the first two weeks of What's the Rule? than…"What's the rule?"

(There is no harm in sitting down with your child the following day and discussing the disturbing behavior that occurred the night before. The method that will be used during this process is discussed in Chapter Eleven, page 146: The Meeting or The Family Meeting.)

Meanwhile, Back at the Ranch

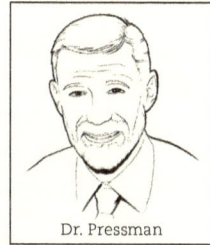
Dr. Pressman

Okay. Julia and Rick have done all the preparation. The saga continues…

Night One: Not Too Dreadful

On the first night, R.J. enjoys the new pre-bedtime routine, goes to bed at 7:00, but gets up at 7:10. Mom and Dad are in the kitchen, sitting at the table, talking and watching the news. R.J. comes into the kitchen. Dad continues to watch TV.

Julia: R.J., What's the rule?

R.J.: I can't sleep. I'm scared!

Julia: [calmly] The rule is that you are in bed at 7:00 for the night.

R.J., surprisingly, goes back into his bedroom. Ten minutes later, he reappears, this time saying that he has to pee.

Dad looks up from the TV and gestures (open palm) toward the bathroom, raising his eyebrows, showing a small smile. (Think headwaiter at an expensive restaurant, elegantly motioning you toward your table.) He does not say a word. R.J. goes to the bathroom and then back into his room.

R.J. is having a hard time getting used to this bedtime routine; it's new and he doesn't really understand it. He doesn't know if it's a "for sure" rule, or a "maybe" rule, so he has to find out. That's called testing. That's what kids do; sometimes, adults do that, too.

After another 10 minutes, he comes out again. He goes into the kitchen; Julia is taking a casserole out of the oven.

Rick: What's the rule?

[R.J. says nothing.]

Rick: The rule is in bed at 7:00 for the night. [He gestures towards R.J.'s bedroom, moving toward it, but R.J. doesn't move. Instead, he walks over to the table and sits down.]

R.J.: I want that. Why do you get to eat that and I had to eat spaghetti? (See red herring, above: Spaghetti is R.J.'s favorite meal.)

Julia puts down the dish and makes the same gesture, moving in the direction of R.J.'s room. He shakes his head, tears starting. Rick goes to the door of R.J.'s room and beckons to him. R.J. gets up and goes to his Dad. Dad nods and looks into R.J.'s room. As R.J. moves in, Dad shuts the door.

Julia has served the salad and poured some iced tea.

Julia: Well, I guess it could be worse!

Rick: Don't say that!

R.J.: [appearing again] I have to go pee.

[Rick starts to say, "You just went!" but stops himself.]

Rick: What's the rule, sweetie?

[R.J. shrugs.]

Rick: The rule is in bed at 7:00 for the night. [He nods, smiling, and gestures toward the bedroom.]

Julia sits down. Rick starts eating his salad. R.J. shuffles off to the bathroom. Sometime later, they hear a flush. R.J. reappears.

R.J.: That looks like good salad. I want some. (Red herring: R.J. hates all raw vegetables; Julia has to hide them in some other food. As a tactic to get to Julia, therefore, it's a smart choice.)

Julia looks at Rick; Rick looks at R.J., gestures smilingly toward his room, and continues to eat. Julia gets up and starts to serve the casserole. R.J. moves between her and the table. She walks around him and puts the plates down. She sits down and begins to eat her dinner.

R.J. starts to cry, but he goes to his room. He slams the door and starts howling. There is the sound of things being thrown. (Red herring. FYI: Before instituting What's the Rule? you might want to remove that valuable collection of antique model cars from Great Grandpa or the 100-year-old bisque doll from Nana; at least put them on a high shelf, out of reach.)

Rick: You said something about worse?

Julia: Oh, shut up! Seriously, I can't eat while this is going on. I feel terrible. Poor R.J.!

Rick: Poor R.J.? Poor Mrs. McKenna! (The downstairs neighbor, who has not always been very neighborly.)

Julia: [laughing] When you put it that way...

The crying and crashing lasts for almost 30 minutes, then stops. It seems as if R.J. has cried himself to sleep. Julia wants to peek in on him; Rick objects.

Julia: What if he's hurt himself?

Rick: He'd come out. Just leave it, Julia. Remember what the doctor said.

Julia: I know, I know. [Sighs] And this is just the first night.

Amazingly, R.J. sleeps through the night. Julia and Rick are ecstatic. One night, and they have the first uninterrupted night's sleep in their own home—ever! They know that they are going to be the first parents to lick this problem in just one night. Hmmm.

Night Two: Fairly Dreadful, but Different

Julia and Rick aren't expecting any major problems on the second night of establishing What's the Rule? but they have vowed to continue the program, in case there are any. R.J. goes to bed without a complaint, and Julia and Rick cannot believe how easy it was. However, within five minutes, R.J. comes out of his bedroom.

R.J.: I have to pee.

Julia: R.J., What's the rule?

[R.J. stands there.]

Julia: The rule is in bed by 7:00 for the night. [She gestures toward the bathroom, then the bedroom.]

R.J. stands and stares at her, then walks slowly to the bathroom. After about 10 minutes, Julia can hear water running and R.J. has not reappeared. She waits another five minutes; Rick is on the phone, so she goes into the bathroom. R.J. is sitting on the toilet lid, running water, and playing with the little paper cups on the sink. Julia calmly turns the water off, squats down, and asks, "Honey, What's the rule?"

[R.J. shrugs.]

Julia: The rule is in bed at 7:00 for the night. [She gestures toward his room.]

R.J. sits on the toilet, swinging his legs. He seems very interested in the feet of his pajamas. Julia has to repress a smile. She crosses her arms, leans against the wall, and waits. In a few minutes, R.J. goes to his room.

From time to time, over the next couple of hours, they hear sounds of talking and singing coming from R.J.'s room. Then there are periods of silence. Julia and Rick find themselves creeping around, trying not to make noise. At some point they realize how silly they are being, and put on a movie.

Too tired to finish the movie, Rick and Julia are in bed and almost asleep, when R.J., hugging Timmy Tiger, knocks softly and comes into their room without waiting for an invitation.

(Big red herring: Both parents feel strongly about privacy. In their home, one does not enter a room without an invitation when the door is closed. This is a tough one to ignore! But—they both remember: focus on one thing at a time. The entering without an invitation can be discussed the next day, or at some later time. Good parents! Also, see "Open Door Policy," Chapter Eleven, page 148.)

R.J.: There are cockroaches in my walls. What if they come out and eat me? (Red herring: he has heard his parents discuss that some people on the second floor had a cockroach problem, and Julia is eternally cockroach vigilant. This is a clever boy!)

Rick: [turning on his bedside lamp] What's the rule, champ?

R.J.: In my room. I know...but the cockroaches!

Rick moves to the doorway and beckons his son. R.J. comes; Rick gestures to his son's bedroom, and then closes his own bedroom door. They can hear the sound of pathetic crying.

Rick: I think you may really have the kid scared with all the talk about the damn roaches.

Julia: Oh, right, Rick. "Killer Cockroaches from Hell! News at 11:00!" Don't blame me, you—roach!

[They both start to laugh.]

Julia: He looked so small and pathetic hugging Timmy.

Rick: [rolling over and hugging her] Don't worry, honey. Timmy will protect him—from the killer cockroaches from hell.

[They eventually fall asleep.]

Night Three: Just Plain Dreadful

Both Rick and Julia are tired, because they did not sleep well the night before. They had very busy days at work but made sure to get home as scheduled. They had no idea what to expect from night three, but they found out pretty quickly.

In order to get home early and have hall running time, Julia had to forego grocery shopping, so she decided to have their favorite Chinese restaurant deliver. R.J. is in his room, playing with his Legos when the food is delivered. As the delivery person leaves, Rick walks in. He kisses Julia and is in the process of taking off his jacket when R.J. bursts into the room.

R.J.: We got done running too early. It was stupid! Yuk! What's that smell?

Rick: And "hello" to you, too.

R.J.: That smells like poops. I'm not eating that crap! (Red Herring already and it's not even bedtime!) He runs back into his room.

[Rick and Julia look at each other, horrified.]

Julia: Crap? Where did he learn that? You don't say crap. I don't say crap—shit sometimes—but never in front of him!

Rick: And "hello" to you, too. Maybe I should go out and come in again?

Julia: Yeah, if you think it would help. He's been like this since I picked him up.

Rick: Did he have a bad day at school?

Julia: Au contraire! Miss Peterson said it was his best day all week. Go figure.

Rick: Well, I'm ready to eat the c-r-a-p whenever you are.

R.J. goes from annoying to angry. At dinner, he refuses to eat his wonton soup, saying it, "tastes like yukky fish." (Red herring: he had never tasted fish, yukky or otherwise.)

Then he spits his favorite beef with broccoli out on the table. "It tastes nasty!" he yells. Julia removes his plate. Julia and Rick continue eating; R.J. plays with his silverware for a while then goes to his room and takes out a puzzle.

During bath time, he dawdles until Julia pulls the plug from the drain, then he smashes his boat on the water, so water splashes all over—especially all over Julia.

He proclaims his video "babyish" and is unable to choose three books for Rick to read. Finally, out of time and patience, Rick puts him to bed, forgetting to take him to the toilet.

R.J., of course, comes running out of the room, yelling, "Daddy is a stupid head. He didn't take me to the potty!"

Rick: [in an undertone to Julia] He's lucky Daddy doesn't crack his head. What is the deal with him tonight?

Julia: What's the rule, R.J.?

R.J.: Daddy didn't take me to the potty and you didn't kiss me. [He bursts into tears.] (Another Big Red Herring: R.J. is correct in saying that Rick didn't take him to the toilet and that Julia didn't kiss him good night. This could be the "straw that breaks the camel's back" for some parents.)

Julia guides R.J. into the bathroom, waits for him, walks him back to his bedroom, and tucks him in—still sobbing. She says the prayer with him—still sobbing—kisses him good night, and turns out his light. He is still crying when she shuts the door.

Fulfilling the Bedtime Contract

Although it may seem as though Julia reinforced unwanted behavior by taking R.J. back to his room and completing the

Stephanie, LICSW

bedtime routine, she didn't. She completed the process that the family had agreed to define as "bedtime routine." She didn't add to it, or give extra attention, or get mad at Rick.

Recognizing that this is a stressful time for the whole family, I really congratulate Julia on keeping her cool and not using Rick's lapse as an excuse to get angry, blow off stream, fix blame, take the opportunity to be "the favorite parent" by sneaking in an extra cuddle, or chuck the whole plan. Kudos to you, Julia.

 **Julia and Rick's Story Continued**

R.J. and Timmy Tiger come out a few minutes later, and just stand, crying, in the doorway of the living room.

Rick: What's the rule, honey? [R.J. continues to cry.]

Rick: The rule is in bed by 7:00 for the night.

R.J. develops hiccups. Rick goes to R.J.'s room and motions for R.J. to come. R.J. lies down on the living room floor and won't move. He cries hysterically and kicks the floor.

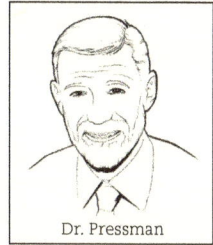

Dr. Pressman

Julia is scared. She signals to Rick to meet her in their room.

Julia: I'm afraid he's going to make himself sick. This is night three, for God's sake. It should be getting easier— not worse! I don't think I can do this, Rick.

Rick: [hugging her] I know. It's awful. But if we go to him now, what will we have taught him? That the next time, he'll have to actually harm himself? I mean, we can't give in to this. He'll never stay in his room if we do.

Julia: I know you're right. But my baby is crying as if his heart will break!

Rick: Well, he's my baby, too, Jules, but that's not despair I hear. He sounds royally pissed! Listen to him!

Julia: [listening] You're right. It's a temper tantrum. Whoa... He really does sound mad! I guess...we should just leave him there?

Rick: Yeah. I'm wiped. How about we just get into bed and watch the game with the volume off?

Julia: Okay. I'm just going to listen to my iPod...and try to forget what a horrible mother I am.

R.J. cries himself out on the living room floor. When Rick goes to the bathroom, he gets a heavy quilt from the couch and covers him.

The next morning, R.J. is all bright eyed and chipper.

R.J.: [announcing to his Mom] I slept in the living room last night. It was like camping out!

Julia: Right. We'll talk about it later.

When Julia picks him up, R.J.'s teacher reports that he told the class about his "camping-out inside," and that the other kids thought it was really cool. She says he is having a good week so far; whatever they are doing must be working. Julia, who is exhausted, just agrees.

Night Four: It Really Works

That night, everything goes like clockwork. R.J. performs his bedtime routine, enjoys his video, chooses his own books, and cuddles with Julia while she reads. He sings along with the special bedtime song, and says his prayers. After both parents kiss him good night, he and Timmy roll over and, apparently, go to sleep.

As soon as R.J. is in bed, his parents have grilled cheese sandwiches and tomato soup, and they go to bed.

Everyone sleeps through the night. It was all Good Nights from then on.

Conclusion

Children are people, and people don't like to change. It is a fact of life, however, that change is not only inevitable, but often desirable. When parents decide to make a big change in the way the family has been operating, it is often threatening to their children. The unfamiliar can be scary, even when the familiar is not working very well.

In the real life story of Julia, Rick, and R.J., we show you how planned change is possible. It isn't always easy or pleasant, but it is doable. We have all trained our children in ways that—with 20/20 hindsight—we wish we hadn't. Learning and then putting What's the Rule? into action is an exemplary way to teach our children with kindness and consistency. Further, it helps us to be better, more thoughtful and more focused parents. Everybody wins—and everybody gets to experience Good Nights. Why wouldn't you?

CHAPTER SEVEN

Another Scenario for Establishing "What's the Rule?"

Stephanie, LICSW

Liz and Ben's Story: Two Children and Living with a Relative

Liz and Ben recently moved in with Liz's mother, Anna. They have been at odds over the lack of structure for their sons at bedtime, which has become more obvious since the family moved in with Liz's mother. Ben and Liz have two sons, Alex and Mark. Alex is 9, and Mark is 5.

Alex is on the hockey team, which has practices five days a week. The games can be during the week, or on weekends. This rigorous schedule makes things hectic for the family. Liz is concerned about disrupting her mother's life more than is necessary, so has wanted to institute the kind of routines she had as a child. Ben has been more focused on "easing the boys" into a new set of rules so soon after the move; he feels that Liz is "too hard on Mark." Because all the adults take turns putting the two children to bed, they all needed to meet and decide what the bedtime rule would be.

Alex didn't really present a problem at bedtime, apart from the usual "can't I just watch one more program?" request about TV time. Mark, however, was whiney, occasionally combative, and was coming into Liz and Ben's bed during the night with increasing frequency.

Framing the Rule

When the adults sat down to make the rule, they realized that they really had no bedtime routine in place for the children. First, they looked at the boys' schedule:

Alex had hockey from September to March. Practice was always over by 7:00 P.M., but weekday games usually didn't finish until 7:15 or 7:30. Mark, who was only five, had no evening activities. However, his bedtime was inappropriately late for a child his age, due to his brother's hockey schedule. They decided that Alex's bedtime would be 9:00 P.M. and that Mark's bedtime would be 7:30 P.M.

The three caregivers decided that Mark should not be brought to Alex's hockey practices or games. Instead, they would trade off who took Alex to hockey. On game nights, Anna would put Alex to bed and both parents would attend the game.

Liz, Ben, and Anna defined bedtime for Alex as, "In bed at 9:00 for the night." They defined bedtime for Mark as, "In bed at 7:30 for the night."

Liz, Ben, and Anna had completed the first step in the process and defined the bedtime rule for their children.

Now let's run the rule through the filter to see if it will work.

THE RULE:

- ◆ Mark: In bed at 7:30 for the night.

- ◆ Alex: In bed at 9:00 for the night.

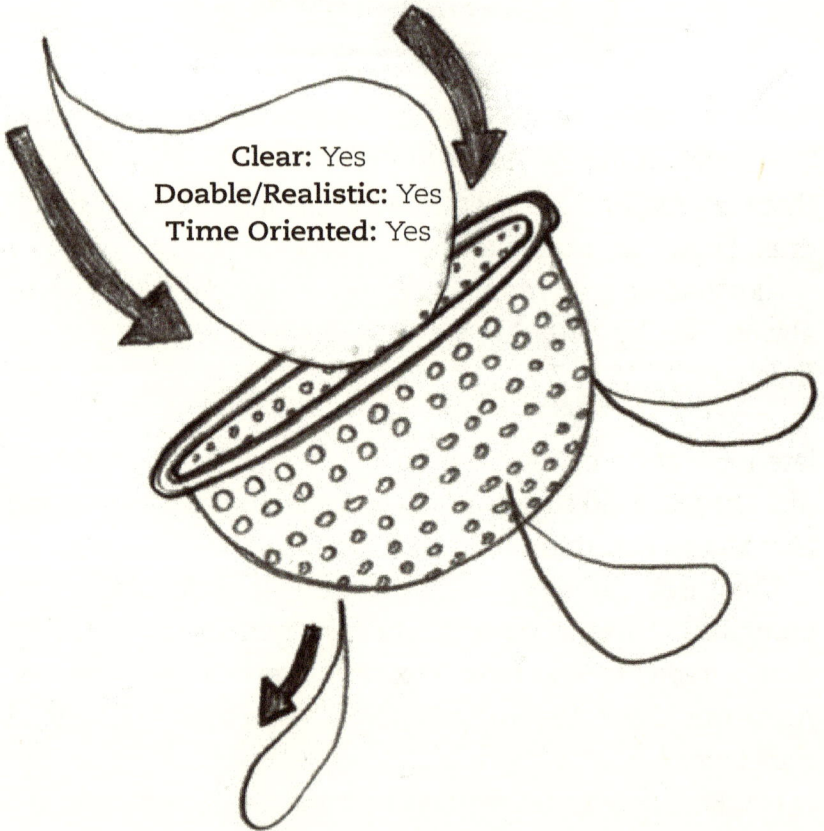

Clear: Yes
Doable/Realistic: Yes
Time Oriented: Yes

2

Deciding When to Implement the Rule

Once the rule has been fully defined and all caregivers are in agreement, it is time to determine when to implement it. Remember that for any rule to meet the criteria in the rule filter, it must be consistent and reinforceable. This is why deciding *when* to implement the rule is extremely important; after it is in place, it will become self-reinforcing. In the beginning, however, you will need to reinforce the rule and be consistent in doing so; hence, the two week commitment on the part of the parents.

Liz and Ben's Story

Initially, all three caregivers wanted to start the new rule the next day. However, after looking at their schedules, they realized that Ben had a company dinner on Friday night that Liz was attending with him. Anna was away for the weekend visiting friends, so they had hired a babysitter.

They were disappointed but realized that starting immediately was not the best idea. Therefore, they decided that
the following week was fine and agreed to start the routine on Monday. Now the rule could be reinforced by the
primary caregivers for the first few weeks, and it would
be consistent.

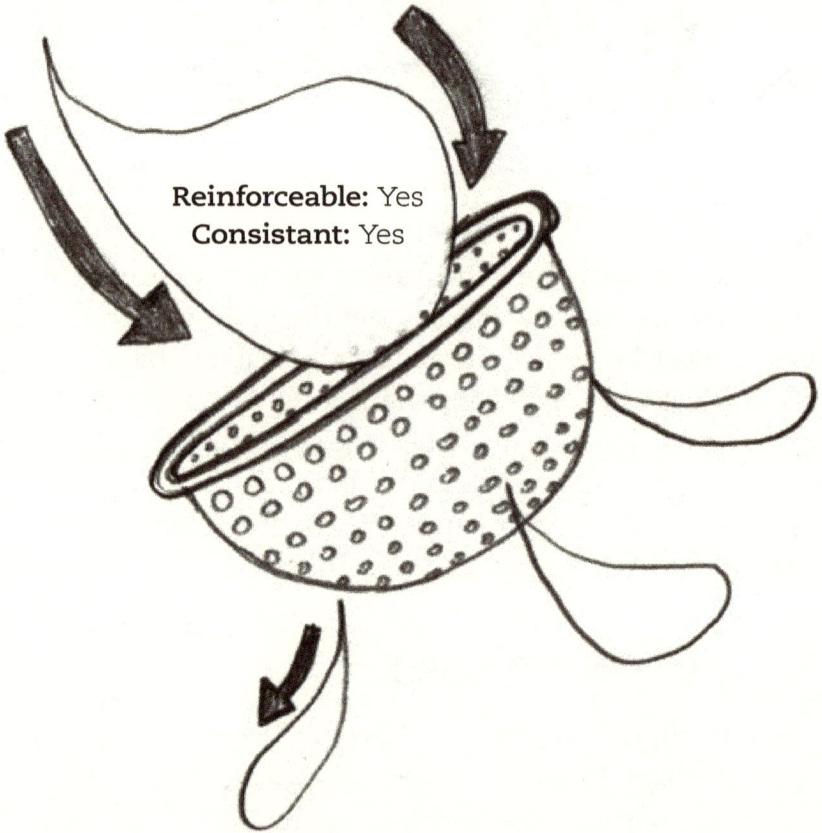

Reinforceable: Yes
Consistant: Yes

3

Establishing
a Bedtime Routine

All three caregivers agreed that Mark's routine would include either a 30-minute video or an age appropriate 30-minute television show followed by a bath, brushing teeth, getting on pajamas, reading three books, and then going to bed. They would begin this routine at 6:30 to have him in bed at 7:30.

Alex's routine would include a shower, brushing teeth, getting on pajamas, 30 minutes of non-violent television, and 20 minutes of reading. Alex's routine would begin at 7:45.

4

Starting
a New
Rule

Liz, Ben, and Anna sit down with both children for a family meeting directly following breakfast on Monday morning. (Great job, the A.M. works best!)

Ben: [to Alex] How old are you now?

Alex: [slightly confused] You don't know? Dad, I'm 9!

Liz: How old is Mark?

Mark: [giggling] FIVE!

Ben: Wow, you guys are so much older than you used to be! Now that you are so much older, there is a new responsibility you're old enough to have. You are going to sleep in your own rooms, all night long.

Liz: [jumping in] We know that bedtime has been a difficult time, so we are going to set this up in a way that is a lot better for everyone. Alex, we are going to have you get your shower out of the way early, brush your teeth, and get in your pj's. After that you get 30 minutes of TV and then Daddy, Grandma, or I will read to you for a while. We thought about starting the *Chronicles of Narnia* books that have been sitting on your bookshelf. We will read a few chapters every night. Or, if you prefer, you can just read quietly to yourself.

Ben: Mark, every night you may watch a special show with Mommy, Daddy, or Grandma and then take a bath, brush your teeth, and put on your pj's. Then we will read three books in your big boy bed.

Liz and Ben: [together] The rule for Alex is in bed at 9:00 for the night. The rule for Mark is in bed at 7:30 for the night. (They have the boys restate the rules, which they are both able to do.)

Liz, Ben, and Anna did a terrific job explaining the rules. They chose the morning, so everyone was rested and alert; they kept the conversation upbeat and happy. Liz briefly acknowledged that things hadn't been going too well. They covered the new bedtime routine and made sure the children understood the new rule. So far, so good.

Let's see what happened with Mark and Alex.

Night One: Pretty Bad

On the first night, Alex does well, but Mark doesn't. He goes to bed at 7:30 but gets up at 7:45. Anna is in her room, Mom is reading, and Dad is watching TV; Alex is in the shower. Mark comes downstairs and sits down in front of the TV.

Ben continues to watch TV.

Liz: [looking up from her book] What's the rule?

Mark: I don't want to go to bed. Nobody else has to!

Liz: [calmly] The rule is in bed at 7:30 for the night.

Mark goes back into his bedroom. A few minutes later he appears again, this time stating, "I'm real thirsty. I need a glass of water. Can you get me some water, Mommy?"

Mom looks up from her book and, smiling, gestures (open hand, palm up) toward the bathroom. She does not say a word. Mark goes to the bathroom and then back into his room.

After another 10 minutes, he comes down again. Now it is Alex's TV time and both parents and Anna are sitting on the couch with Alex watching his special show.

Mark: Hey, why does Alex get TV? I want TV!

Ben: What's the rule?

[Mark says nothing.]

Ben: The rule is in bed at 7:30 for the night. [He gets up and moves toward Mark's room; he gestures for Mark to follow him. Mark follows; Dad shuts the door to Mark's room and returns to the living room.]

Almost immediately, Mark reappears. Ben does the same thing, but this time, Mark doesn't follow him. Instead, he walks over to the TV and sits down right in front of it.

Red Herring:
Alex's Special TV Time Interruption

Dr. Pressman

Remember, this is Alex's special TV time. You can see how this situation could quickly spiral out of control.

In this situation, parents have a couple of options. The first option is to pause the program (if possible) and gesture toward the bedroom. No one—including Alex—speaks to Mark. After a minute or two of silence, he will get the hint. Turning the television off is even better; that's more difficult in this particular situation, as this is Alex's time.

The second option is to move Alex to another location, if there is a second TV. In this case, Liz and Ben have a TV in their room.

Liz and Ben's Story Continued

Liz and Ben decide to pause Alex's program. Liz gives Alex a signal (shaking her head and putting her index finger to her lips—the universal sign for "be quiet") while Ben interposes himself between Mark and the TV.

Ben: Mark, What's the rule?

[Mark shakes his head, pulls up his knees, and hides his face on his knees.]

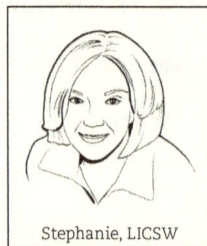

Stephanie, LICSW

Ben: The rule is in bed by 7:30 for the night.

Liz gets up and takes Alex into her room, where—not very happily—he resumes watching his program. In reality, he has only missed a couple of commercials; when he realizes this, he feels better.

Meanwhile, back in the living room:

Mark doesn't move. Ben goes into the bedroom with Liz and Alex and shuts the door.

After a few minutes, Mark starts banging on his parents' door.

Alex: Jeez!

Liz: (shushes him, and gives him a little pat) Stay cool, honey. This is going to be going on for a few nights, but it will get better. I promise.

[Alex nods, caught up again in his program. Ben opens the door and leaves, shutting it behind him.]

Ben: What's the rule, sweetie?

[Mark doesn't answer; he is crying.]

Ben: The rule is in bed by 7:30 for the night. [He walks past Mark, to Mark's room. He beckons Mark. Mark comes, crying. Ben leads Mark into his room, then leaves and shuts the door.]

Mark has a huge tantrum. He screams at the top of his lungs. His parents ignore him, his grandmother stays in her room, and Alex turns up the volume and finishes his program. His mom takes him to his room and gets him settled in bed with his book. Ben comes in to kiss him good night. Alex is in for the night.

Mark continues his tantrum for over an hour; it includes jerking his door open, running to his parents' room and banging and kicking on their door, and then running back to his room and slamming the door.

Liz goes to her mother's room to see how she is doing; Anna has fallen asleep.

Eventually Mark exhausts himself, and the noise stops. Ben and Liz are tense and upset.

Ben: I don't know if I can take this. I don't even want to see what our door looks like. The kid is wrecking your Mom's house!

Liz: She doesn't seem too upset; she's asleep. Thank God! Poor Mom!

Ben: I have to say, your mother has been a rock through all this. My parents would've skinned Mark alive by now.

Liz: Don't forget—she had to deal with my brother. He made Mark look like an angel.

Ben: Really? I didn't know. How'd you turn out so good?

Liz: Oh, so now I'm good? I've been "the bad parent" for weeks!

Ben: Let's not start. Mark's just—Mark. He's our kid—for better or worse. We have to deal with him. Do you forgive me for being such a jerk?

Liz: Maybe. Make it worth my while, and I'll consider it.

Although Mark's tantrum behavior was horrific, he did not come into his parents' bed that night. Neither parent slept well, however. Liz was anxious and still angry at both Mark and Ben; Ben was furious with Mark.

Night Two: Pretty Bad, but Different

Liz and Ben aren't looking forward to the second night of What's the Rule? They are both feeling tired and tense, but the pre-bed routines go smoothly. Mark goes to bed without a complaint, and Liz and Ben can't believe how easy it was. Within five minutes though, Mark comes out, holding Mr. Bear.

Mark: I have to pee.

Liz: What's the rule, honey?

[Mark just sticks his thumb in his mouth and looks at her.]

Liz: The rule is in bed at 7:30 for the night.

Liz smiles and starts to move toward the bathroom, beckoning. Mark stands and stares at her, then walks slowly to the bathroom. Liz waits outside the bathroom door. When Mark comes out, she walks toward his room and gestures for him to go in. He starts to cry and throws himself at her legs. Liz—feeling like a cruel and callous mother—untangles him, gives him a gentle nudge into his room, and shuts the door.

Liz returns to the living room, where Alex and Ben are watching TV. She sits beside Ben, puts her arm around him and whispers, "You're up next."

A few minutes later, Mark and Mr. Bear come in and sit on the floor, in front of the TV. Ben, trying not to look irritated, turns off the TV, and stands in front of Mark. Alex goes directly to his parents' room and turns on the TV; Liz stays on the couch. She picks up a magazine, and leafs through it.

Ben: What's the rule, big guy?

Mark: [throwing Mr. Bear at his father, then lying on his stomach, screaming] I hate you! You're a bad daddy! You love Alex more than me. Why? Why do you hate me? YOU LOVE ALEX AND YOU HATE ME!

The Mommy's Perspective

Mommy Rebecca

In this situation, it goes against every parental instinct not to rush to a child and assure him that he is loved. Saying nothing—allowing that statement to go unchallenged—seems like the wrong thing to do. After all, as good parents, don't we want the one thing our children can always count on to be our love for them? Of course we do! That's why this situation is so hard—because what *seems* right is NOT the right thing to do.

Red Herrings Revisited

Dr. Pressman

We call this kind of intervention *counterintuitive* because not reassuring a child of our love goes against our parental intuition and instincts. In this situation, reassuring Mark will be following the red herring. It will certainly make Mark feel better at that moment. However, it will also teach him that all he has to say is, "You don't love me as much as Alex," and the rule—any rule—will go out the window. That will not be a good or helpful thing for Mark to learn; it gives him too much power—power that can be used to undermine rules that are made *for his benefit!* Mark may be unhappy now, but when he is able to go to bed and stay in his room all night, he will be a happier and more confident boy.

That's why doing what *feels* wrong can sometimes be the right thing to do. Remember, this particular event is not a sprint; it's a long-distance run. At the end of this particular event, everybody in the house is a winner.

Back to Night Two

Stephanie, LICSW

Ben: The rule is in bed by 7:30 for the night. [He moves toward Mark's room, gesturing for Mark to follow him.]

Mark continues his tantrum. Liz and Ben go upstairs. Alex has finished his program. Tonight, he wants Liz to read to him, so she cuddles with him while she reads. Alex is very tired and falls asleep on her after 15 minutes. She tucks him in, kisses him, turns out the light, and leaves his room.

Ben: Can I go in and say good night to Alex?

Liz: He fell asleep while I was reading, poor guy.

Ben: Do you think I'd wake him if I went in?

Liz: I doubt that a rock concert would wake him. Go ahead.

Ben goes in and retucks Alex's blankets. He can hear Mark, but just barely. He kisses his son, then sits in Alex's chair and watches him sleep. He falls asleep but wakes up when Liz comes in to get him.

Ben: [back in their room] How long was I asleep?

Liz: Just a few minutes. I only went in to drop off his laundry—some of his shorts got mixed in with yours. You must really be tired; I've never seen you fall asleep sitting up—in a desk chair, no less!

Ben: I think it's called escape. What's Mark doing?

Liz: I don't know. He got quiet when I went into Alex's room. Maybe he fell asleep in the living room.

Ben: Well, I'm not checking! He can sleep on the floor all night.

Liz: I know. I'm so mad at him, but he breaks my heart. What he said.... [She sits on the bed and bursts into tears.] This is so awful. I know Stephanie told us it would be, but it's different when it's your baby!

Ben sits beside her. He doesn't know what to say. He puts his arm around her, and she cries into his shoulder. Ben feels like crying, too.

Mark bangs on the door, runs in, and climbs into the bed. He is crying, "I can't find Mr. Bear!" Then he looks at Liz, "Mommy, why are you crying?"

Liz just shakes her head and keeps crying. Mark looks at his father. Ben kisses Liz on the top of her head, walks out of the room, and beckons Mark. They go into the living room and retrieve Mr. Bear from the mantle, where Ben had put him. They walk back to Mark's room.

Ben: What's the rule, Mark?

[Mark hugs his bear and goes over to his bed. He gives Ben an angry look.]

Ben: The rule is in bed at 7:30 for the night.

[Ben leaves, shutting the door.]

Mark stays in his room, but they can hear him talking loudly to his stuffed animals, saying, "Mean Daddy! I hate Daddy!" and other things about Daddy.

Liz wipes her tears. She says, "Better you than me." Ben is not amused.

They get ready for bed, turn out the lights, and are almost asleep when Mark quietly opens the door and gets into bed on Liz's side.

Coming into Bed with the Parents: Lights On!

A child crawling into the parent's bed is a huge problem. There is only one way to handle it. Get out of bed, turn on the light, and ask, "What's the rule?" State the rule, then gesture toward his bedroom. The first time he gets up, you may need to walk him back to the room, but do not speak to him and do not tuck him in. Simply gesture him into the room and leave.

Dr. Pressman

If he attempts to sneak in again, turn on the light, and ask "What's the rule?" If he responds with a shrug, or an "I don't know" or a red herring, repeat the rule. This time move and gesture toward the bedroom where he sleeps—do not say another word.

I have known parents who had to stand, nodding and gesturing toward the child's room, for two full minutes before their child moved. Don't worry, he will get the point. When you turn on the light, it takes away the comfy cozy feel of sneaking into bed with Mom and Dad.

Mark may come out of his room 20 more times that night. He may crawl into bed with his parents and throw a tantrum that wakes up the house. However, this problem really *will* resolve itself within three or four days if you remember that the only things that are spoken are "What's the rule?" and the answer to that question. Afterward, only nonverbal cues are given.

Night Two Continued

Liz sits up, turns on the light, and gets out of bed.

Liz: What's the rule?

Stephanie, LICSW

[Mark doesn't move; he just squinches his eyes shut.]

Liz: The rule is in bed for the night at 7:30.

[Mark looks at her, and she gestures to his room.]

Mark starts to sniffle, but he gets out of bed. He ver-r-r-ry slowly shuffles to his room. Liz closes the bedroom door, gets back into bed, and turns off the light.

Ben: Nice job, honey.

Some time later—after Ben and Liz have fallen asleep—Liz rolls over and feels a small body at the foot of the bed. She feels torn; she knows what she *should* do, but she doesn't want to do it. If she gets up and turns on the light, Ben will wake up, she will be fully awake, and she'll have a tough time going back to sleep. Maybe, she thinks, I can just pretend I didn't wake up and leave him there. It's not my fault if I don't *know* he's here!

But Liz remembers Stephanie saying, "You need to be consistent. Your boys are smart and resourceful and tenacious. They want things to stay the same; they will resist change—even if it's good. You need to be smarter, more resourceful, and more determined than they are. Remember: you're going through a few nights of misery to get years of uninterrupted sleep. Hang in there."

Inwardly groaning, Liz rolls over, turns on the light, and gets out of bed. Ben says, "What the..." and then sees Mark. Ben gets out of bed.

Ben: What's the rule?

Mark: No. I have a pain. I'm sick.

Ben: The rule is in bed at 7:30 for the whole night.

Mark: My tummy hurts. And my throat.

Ben turns the light on, goes to the bedroom door, and beckons Mark. Liz nudges him out of bed, gets out herself, and turns on her light. Mark starts to wail.

Ben: What's the rule, Mark?

Mark: Mommy. I'm sick. Don't make me do this.

Ben: The rule is in bed for the night at 7:30.

Mark stands immobile, looking at his Dad. After what seems an eternity, but is really only a minute or so, Mark sighs and—a picture of abject dejection—goes to his room. He turns, shuts his door—with force less than a slam but more than a shut.
Ben goes back to bed; they turn off the lights.
Mark opens and then slams his bedroom door. Mark starts screaming.
Both Ben and Liz are wide awake.

Liz: Do you think he might really be sick?

Ben: I don't think he's dying. I think he's pissed. If he pukes, we'll clean it up and put him back to bed.

Liz: That's harsh!

Ben: He's fine. He's just stubborn...and loud. Try to go to sleep, Liz.

A few minutes later, Alex knocks on the door and comes in.

Alex: What's the deal with Mark? There was a loud noise, and now he's screaming. Is he okay?

Liz: He's fine, honey. He just doesn't like the new bedtime rules.

Alex: Can't you make him shut up? I'm tired; I have a math test and a game tomorrow. I want to sleep.

Ben: Put your pillow over your head, champ. He'll quiet down eventually. We just need to ignore him and he'll stop. Go back to bed.

Liz: Alex, whatever he does, please don't talk to him. Don't go in or anything, promise?

Ben: What's the rule for you, pal?

Alex: Yeah, okay. Whatever. [Under his breath, "I'd like to punch him!" Alex leaves.]

Ben: I'd kind of like to punch him myself.

Liz: That makes three of us. I hope Mom doesn't wake up!

Mark cries for 20 minutes, and then falls asleep. Ben and Liz eventually fall asleep, also.

Night Three: Hope Springs Eternal

On the third night, Alex has a game, so Anna puts Mark to bed. When Ben, Liz, and Alex get home, she reports that Mark was "a little angel" and "went to bed without a peep."

Alex showers, they all watch TV with him, and then they all head upstairs. Liz reads to Alex and tucks him in. He is asleep before she even turns out his light. By the time she gets to her room, Ben is already in bed, reading.

Ben: I'm really beat. Do you think he'll stay in bed tonight?

Liz: God, I hope so. I don't know how much more of this I can take.

She turns off her light immediately after getting into bed. "I'm too tired to read."

They both fall asleep. After an hour, Liz hears the bedroom door open. Mark starts to get into bed. Liz jumps out of bed, turns on the light, and asks, "What's the rule?"

Mark stops, looks at her, then turns around and goes back to his room. Liz shuts the bedroom door, turns out the light, and after an hour, falls asleep.

Mark stays in his room for the rest of the night.

Night Four: It Really Does Work!

When Liz kisses Mark good night, he asks, "Can I watch TV with Alex tonight?"

Liz asks, "What's the rule?"

Mark sighs, hugs his bear, rolls over, and goes to sleep.

Night Five

No problems. There are nothing but Good Nights from now on.

Conclusion

We have given you the blow-by-blow illustration of using What's the Rule? in two families: one with a single child and one with two children and a further complicating factor—living in someone else's home. Both families saw the end of problems in four nights. This isn't a magic number; the cases we chose happened to work out that way. You may have no problems at all or virtually no problems by the second night. You may be the extremely rare example of having testing go longer than that. Regardless of how many nights it takes, What's the Rule? will solve bedtime problems, permanently. And don't forget, *Matilda and Maxwell's Good Night* will help your children with the transition.

PART THREE

All Kinds of
INTERESTING
THINGS
Good Parents NEED
TO KNOW!

CHAPTER EIGHT

Personalities and Behaviors

True Confession of a Child Psychologist

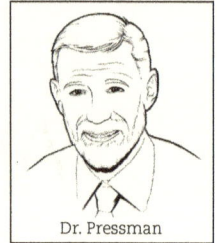

Dr. Pressman

None of us are perfect parents. I confess that I was an anxious parent. I would go to the pediatrician with my wife and our first child and—with great concern—describe behaviors that were totally normal! I still remember asking, "Why does Sarah shake her hands back and forth when she gets excited?" At the time, my daughter, Sarah, was nine months old.

At another visit, I asked the doctor, "Why does Sarah look so worried all the time?" The doctor replied, "Go look in the mirror. If I was lying in a crib looking up at your anxious face, I'd be worried too." He was pointing out—with good humor—that my daughter was just responding to the messages I was sending. What a revelation!

The good news is that we don't need to be perfect all the time. However, it helps to maintain a degree of calmness and thoughtfulness when dealing with our children's big personalities. The example I gave of my daughter reflecting my anxiety is actually an example of something called *modeling*. Our children learn behaviors by modeling or copying our behavior. For example, when a child sees his parent get frustrated, become angry, and start yelling, he is being taught how to deal *ineffectively* with stress. If the same child sees his parent make reasonable demands and react calmly, he will learn how to deal with stress quite well.

This concept has obvious implications for the setting up of a new bedtime routine. When parents are calm, kind, firm, and focused, the "learning curve"—that is, the amount of time children require to learn something—will be shorter. Parents are modeling the bedtime behavior they wish to teach their children. That's what we need to focus on. Makes sense, doesn't it?

True Confession of a Mommy

What's the Word on the Street? FOCUS!

Okay, I confess! My name is Rebecca, and I am a Sesame Street[1] Mother. There. I feel better.

Mommy Rebecca

I can absolutely understand why it is so hard for all of us to focus on just teaching our child one thing at a time. I want Hunter to be assertive, but I want her to be polite and say "please" and "thank you." I also want her to sit politely through dinner and eat all her vegetables. I want her to keep the water in the bathtub instead of splashing it onto the floor. And, if I happen to say something inappropriate in front of her, I definitely don't want her to repeat it! Phew!

As a parent, I feel all the pressures of my paid work, and then my biggest job, which is my unpaid work—being a wife, mother, housekeeper, nurse, chauffeur, judge, advocate, chef, and entertainer—especially entertainer.

I want so many things for my daughter and my son. I know that I can't teach them everything that's important to me all at once. As a member of Sesame Street-Mothers-No-Longer-Anonymous, I understand I have to take it one task at a time, one day at a time, one behavior at a time, one rule at a time. I can do that. Focus. Focus is the word on the street.

Confession of a Clinical Social Worker

I suppose it's best to just spit it out. I love the movie *Who Framed Roger Rabbit*.[2] I saw it three times in the theatre and bought it as soon as it came out on video; now I own the DVD.

Stephanie, LICSW

In the movie, there were some unsavory characters out to get Roger Rabbit. They were able to trick him into revealing his hiding place because they knew his weakness: he was totally unable to ignore a particular sound pattern. In this case, it was: "shave and a haircut [pause] two bits." When the bad guys tapped out the rhythm "shave and a haircut" they stopped before "two bits." Roger could not let the pattern go unfinished; he was *compelled* to tap out the last two sounds, "two bits," and they caught him. (Maybe you had to see it?)

I use this story with patients, because it demonstrates how not being able to focus on one thing—in our case, on a single behavior called bedtime behavior—can really catch you up. Roger wasn't able to focus on staying hidden; he was distracted by the red herring of "shave and a haircut," and it did him in. When you're trying to establish a new rule or routine, you have to develop a kind of tunnel vision; that is, you must not pay attention to any behaviors that may occur, *other than the ones you want*. This is crucial!

And it is really difficult for many of us to ignore truly horrid behavior—such as those listed in Chapter Six, page 58. Like Roger Rabbit, we feel a compulsion to DO something, right now. If you give in to that impulse, you lose. When your personality ("I can't let this go!") engages in a contest with your child's personality ("She can't make me do this—I'll just sit here and scream!") What's the Rule? and any positive bedtime training is doomed.

[2] *Who Framed Roger Rabbit*. Directed by Robert Zemeckis. Los Angeles: Touchstone Pictures, 1988. Motion Picture.

Parental Personalities and Behaviors

Because we all have personalities, we all have certain traits, beliefs, or patterns that can act like sand traps on a golf course. Once we fall into the trap, it takes a bit of effort to get out; it's better to avoid the trap altogether, as any golfer can tell you. These personality traits (or personality traps!) are often the very reason we feel "stuck" in a negative situation with our children. Here are three examples of different personalities; are you one of them?

Dr. Pressman

Sympathetic/Vicarious: Sympathy is an admirable trait in human beings. However, when we, as parents, over-identify with the psychological pain that a child may be experiencing during the learning process—as in a new bedtime routine—it can stop us from following through with it. This means that we will have to start the whole process all over again at some later time, and—because of how our child trained *us* the first time—it will be much harder and take far longer.

Sometimes, the sympathetic parent may actually be living vicariously through his child. Therefore, when the child is hurt or disappointed, it is almost as if it happened to the parent himself. Indeed, the parent may take the less-than-happy experiences of his child more seriously than his child does! This can create problems down the line, as the child will learn not to confide in his parent in the fear that the parent will overreact. (See Chapter Ten, page 121.)

Guilty/Indulgent: This occurs when a parent feels a sense of guilt about something that has happened in the child's life. An example of this could be something as big as a divorce or something as small as missing a soccer game that day. The problem is that we, as parents, find ourselves trying to "make up" for the guilt in ways that actually do more harm than good—such as letting our child sleep with us.

This is a case of "teaching" a child something that can become destructive. Once a child figures out that when we feel guilty we give in/bribe/indulge, she can use that knowledge to manipulate us. That's inappropriate power to give a child; it's confusing and damaging and sets up a pattern than can be hard to break. (See Chapter Ten, page 124; you met their 2-year-old daughter, Emma, in Chapter Three).

Overanxious/Overprotective: Anxiety and worry are a fact of life for all parents. It's par for the course. Sometimes, parents are more anxious or fearful regarding the safety and health of their child than is reasonable. This can happen because of a serious illness that occurred during the child's lifetime or simply because we have an overactive imagination. Nonetheless, the outcome is that we let our emotions and fears get in the way of our parenting. The overly protective parent often "protects" the child from learning experiences that will give him self-confidence, like staying in his room all night. (See Chapter Ten, page 126; their 10-year-old son, Ethan, was introduced in Chapter Three).

Conclusion

What's the Rule? is about focusing on positive change, but change is stressful. Any change, be it good (like winning the lottery) or not so good (like losing a job) causes stress. Instituting a bedtime routine is change; by definition, it will be stressful. That's why it is so important that all the adults involved are on the same page before you start the technique. It's going to be stressful for you and your child, so you—the parent(s)—need to be focused, determined, and united.

Remember that this is not a contest of wills—who can outlast the other—although, at times, it may feel that way! This is a technique that establishes a helpful guide for behavior, so everyone in the house has a pleasant evening and a good sleep. Over time, and with consistent reinforcement, this new bedtime behavior becomes a habit. So, stick with it. Avoid the personality traps. Focus. Go team!

Don't forget, we have a book designed for your child that will be a big help to both of you. *Matilda and Maxwell's Good Night* is a fun way to both introduce and reinforce the new bedtime routine.

CHAPTER NINE

Classic Stoppers and Starters

The Mommy's Perspective

Mommy Rebecca

All mothers want to protect and nurture their babies. That is what makes us mommies. Sometimes, despite our best intentions, we go overboard. My daughter was constantly sick her first year. As a new mother, it was terrifying for me. I wanted her to be in playgroups with other children and to socialize, but at the same time, I was uncomfortable exposing her unnecessarily to germs! As time went on, it became apparent that I was overprotecting my daughter by trying to raise her in such a sheltered environment—almost like a bubble.

Now, she goes to music classes, playgroups, and other activities. She has lots of colds and runny noses. Groan. But—she's a happy, outgoing kid with tons of confidence (too much, I sometimes think!). What's a mommy to do?

The Stopper of Guilt and Fear

Stephanie, LICSW

It's finally time to set aside those old demons that have been keeping you from allowing your child to separate from you. Many parents have suffered through their children's severe illness while those children were young; some have a chronic, perhaps debilitating condition. In many of these cases, parents have been involved in a nightly vigil—watching over their child for fear that something would happen and they would not be there to save their baby. At these fearful times, children are often moved into the parental bed. This creates a huge problem!

Amanda's Story: Guilt and Fear Personified

Amanda looked every inch the successful attorney that she was. Her well-tailored suit did a good job of softening her extreme thinness, and her carefully applied make-up helped mask the deep circles under her eyes. Amanda was 38 years old, yet looked at least five years older. She entered counseling with symptoms of anxiety and depression; her reason for seeking help, however, was her daughter, Merri. "She hasn't had anything like a normal life. Now, when she could have one, she has no social skills and no interests. She is afraid of literally everything—from trains to ants to dogs to strangers to new foods. She won't try to ride a bike. She has never had a friend over, or gone to anyone else's house to play. It's... abnormal. She has no life, except for school and me. I have work and her. I feel so guilty...and resentful, Stephanie. I want things to be different."

"I'm...just done," she continued. "I'm always exhausted, always worried, always distracted. I feel so hopeless—and that makes me feel like a bad person. I don't see how I can change anything.... I really care about my clients and their families...they deserve my best effort. But I'm always afraid, anxious. My daughter, she's 11 now, she's come close to dying so many times...I don't know...if only I could sleep for about a year."

Amanda was a single mother. Her daughter, Merri, was born with a congenital birth defect that necessitated seven operations before Merri's first birthday. Amanda had to return to work full time when Merri was 14 months old. Although she located a daycare provider who was a CNA (Certified Nursing Assistant), she still found that she worried all day long about her daughter and felt enormously guilty about leaving her in daycare.

When asked about sleeping arrangements, she recounted that when Merri was a baby, Amanda lay awake listening to the baby monitor; she had to get up frequently to check on her daughter. At least two or three times a year, she had to rush Merri to the hospital for emergency care, so she could never really relax in the knowledge that her daughter would stay safe through the night. She eventually moved the crib into her room, so she could get some sleep.

When Merri was old enough to go into her own room, Amanda would stay with her until she went to sleep. When she went back to her own bed and fell asleep, Merri would seem to sense her absence and cry until she came back. After a few nights of trying to get her daughter to stay in her own bed alone, guilt won out. Merri has essentially slept with her mother for 11 years. Amanda cannot remember having an unbroken night's sleep for 11 years.

Now a reasonably healthy pre-adolescent, Merri has no friends other than the three younger children at her after school care, has never gone to anyone's house to play, never hung out at the mall with other kids. She suffers from what is called *panphobia*—fear of everything. Her mother is chronically sleep deprived, too thin, and being treated for anxiety and depression. But—she can't bring herself to insist that Merri stay in her room at night.

The Boy in the Plastic Bubble Syndrome

Rebecca's account of The Mommy's Perspective, above, is a wonderful example of parents trying to accommodate both ends of the spectrum at once. At one end is keeping your child safe, healthy, protected. At the other end is allowing her to grow, explore, learn—and get sick, injured, scared, rejected, and the all the other conditions we humans must face.

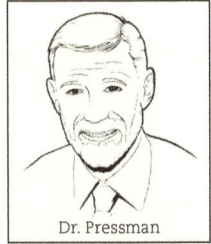
Dr. Pressman

One of the stories I frequently tell patients is Henry the Bubble Boy and Danny the Street Kid. Henry had a poor immune system, so his parents raised him in a big plastic bubble where he was protected from germs and contact with other dangerous things (like the bathroom, the family car, the front yard, friends—you get the picture.) He was totally and completely safe.

Danny's house was on the south side of town and considered a tough neighborhood. Every day his parents sent him out of his house to play and fend for himself. Sometimes he got into scrapes with other boys and came home with cuts and bruises; for the first five or six years, it seemed like he always had a cold or a runny nose.

Both children are now in their teens. Which child do you believe will grow up feeling more self-confident?

Because Henry never had the opportunity to learn that he could deal with the world, he didn't learn self-confidence or experience the pride of independence. Danny may have taken a few hard knocks, but he learned early in life to rely on himself. What all good parents hope for, of course, is to be able to give our child chances to learn self-reliance through a strategy that we can—somewhat—control.

Mothering vs. Smothering

The common thread running through many of the stories we hear is that the parents feel they are *protecting* their children by allowing them to sleep with them. They feel terribly guilty about insisting that their children sleep on their own. They believe that by allowing their children to be comforted by this nighttime closeness, they are somehow lessening the impact of other factors that may not be good in their child's life—poor school performance, lack of friends, absence of a parent through divorce or death, etc. These good parents actually feel that by letting their child have the physical closeness of a parent during the night, they are adding an extra layer of safety and protection that their child can carry with them through the day.

Stephanie, LICSW

In fact, it's quite the opposite. By not setting healthy boundaries for their child at bedtime, they are contributing to their child's feelings of fear and insecurity. They are compounding the child's problems by depriving him of the opportunity to develop confidence in himself and his abilities. Perhaps a more accurate word than *protecting* would be *smothering*.

Relative Wisdom

My father used to say, "There's no sense in worrying that bad things will happen; they will. All the worrying in the world won't prevent them, but it can sure ruin your 'right now.'" My father was correct.

Allowing your kids to disrupt your evening, leave their rooms, and cause nighttime chaos does not insulate them from hurt or pain. It only causes lots of problems and prevents you from getting a good night's sleep.

Calm evenings lead to restful sleep; restful sleep leads to happier and more productive days. The methods outlined in *Good Night* lead to psychologically healthy and rested children and parents.

The Stopper of Change

Laura and James's Story: The War at Home

Laura and James came into their first session distraught.

"I'm so tired and discouraged. Right about now, I wish he'd go back to Iraq!" Laura said.

"It was easier there, trust me!" James agreed. "It made sense. My men did what I told them. Here, nobody does what I tell them—they don't even listen. I feel like everything I do is wrong. At least there, I could count on five hours of sleep; here, I'm lucky to grab three or four. "

At that, Laura giggled. "I don't want you gone, James; I'm so grateful that you're back in one piece." She grabbed his hand, and then added, "But you don't—or won't—understand. Chip and I had our own way of doing things, and it worked. I never had one problem at night before you came back with all your 'rules' and 'my little soldier' crap. Oops—sorry. But it's true. He was a happy, confident little boy, and now he's a…"

"Brat!" James said.

"Do you see what I mean?" Laura asked, tears in her eyes. "It's his way or the highway."

When Laura and James were married right after he graduated from college, they knew that he would have to serve his two years of active duty. James had gone through college with the help of the United States Army, and he was ready to pay back his debt. Both he and Laura thought they knew what they were facing, and both were prepared for two years of separation.

When Laura got pregnant on their honeymoon, they knew they could handle it. Laura worked in a daycare center, so she could take the baby with her if she had to continue working. James was deployed to Iraq just before the baby was born.

Laura did it all on her own. Little James, Jr. looked so much like his father that he was promptly nicknamed Chip, as in, "chip off the old block." Laura went back to work and was able to take Chip with her. The two years of active duty turned into four years for James. In the first four years of Chip's life, he spent a total of five months with his father. Laura was his whole world—and he was hers.

During that time, Laura and Chip established a routine that worked for them. Because they were together all the time, they had a relaxed way of doing things. With no one else's wants or needs to consider, they did what they felt like, when they felt like it. If they wanted peanut butter and jelly sandwiches for breakfast, that's what they had. Lots of nights, they ate cereal in front of the TV, watching Chip's Elmo videos. Sometimes bath time was at night, others it was in the morning.

When Chip got sleepy, Laura would carry him into bed, and read or sing him to sleep. He liked the light left on, so it was. Occasionally, he would get up at night and crawl in bed with her, but not too often. If Laura wanted Chip to get some extra sleep in the morning—no problem! She could just take him to daycare in his pj's, and he could eat breakfast with the other kids.

"When I got the news that James was on his way home, it was the happiest day of my life!" Laura exclaimed. "I told Chip, 'Daddy's coming home; now we can be a real family.' We even baked a cake—Chip helped. I thought all my prayers had been answered, and now life would be perfect."

But, when James came home to stay, the nighttime troubles started. For the first couple of days, it was great; Laura and Chip stayed home with Daddy, and it was a family honeymoon—breakfasts in bed, pizza in front of the TV, and just getting reacquainted. After three days, however, the honeymoon was over.

James had definite ideas about how a family should be run. Stability and discipline were of primary importance, and he was determined to get his new family into disciplined order.

At nighttime, the house became a war zone. Laura often didn't get home until 5:30 or 5:45, but James wanted his "little soldier" fed, bathed, read to, and in bed—lights off, door closed—by 7:00. This was a complete change in routine, with disastrous results.

Chip felt abandoned and frightened. He was being shut away from his mother—in the dark. Laura had never left Chip in a dark room, choosing to leave his light on. When James started to put him to bed, he insisted on "lights out!" Chip preferred his mother; he wanted her to be in his room and read and sing to him. James was hurt that his son was rejecting him and angry at Laura for "babying" Chip.

Laura couldn't bear to hear Chip crying in his room and was furious with James. Every night, Chip would be out of his room, back in his room, until he cried himself to sleep. It got so tense that Chip would start to cry when he heard his bath water running, because that signaled the beginning of bedtime.

Some nights, Laura just couldn't help herself; she would slip out of bed and go into Chip's room and hold him until he fell asleep.

Laura was miserable; she felt like she was being torn in half. She loved her husband and wanted him to have a good relationship with his son. She had hoped to recapture the closeness they shared before he was deployed. But, although she was willing to concede that some changes had to be made, she resented James' superior attitude. She had raised their son all by herself for four years, and he was a happy, outgoing, confident, popular kid. Now, he was a clingy, unhappy, insecure little boy who was starting to act out during the day.

Half of the time she felt angry at James for being so rigid; angry at Chip for being so uncooperative; angry at herself for being a failure as a wife and as a mother. The other half, she longed to have Chip all to herself again and have the happy, uncomplicated life they had shared. She missed her cheery baby and the relaxed and confident way she used to feel. Nighttimes used to be the best part of the day; now they were a waking nightmare.

As for James, for four years he had lived for the day he could return to his wife and son. He was so sure that they would have the life they had dreamed of, planned for, counted on. It seemed that he had left one war only to return to another.

The Stopper of Denial

Kelly and Tiffany: The Weekend Away

Kelly and Tiffany walked into their first session looking hopeless. They recounted a recent weekend they spent with another couple in their vacation home. Both couples had a 2 year old and 4 year old. The weekend, however, quickly turned sour when Kelly and Tiffany's boys kept the whole house up during the night.

They explained to the other couple that their kids might be coming down with a cold, were just scared, were thirsty, had to go to the potty, were upset that the blanket fell off the bed, and so on and so on. They were able to come up with an explanation for every time their kids woke up the house.

The next day when their children acted up and had tantrums, Kelly and Tiffany explained that their sons were just overtired because they had not slept well the night before.

Tiffany said she felt more exhausted from the lying than from the lack of sleep. The truth was, her kids were always like this, and she felt embarrassed by their behavior in front of her friends.

What Are You Teaching and *How* Are You Teaching It?

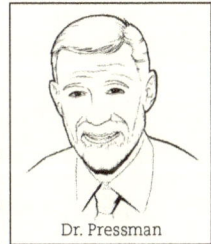
Dr. Pressman

It's important to ask yourself: *What* am I really teaching and *how* am I teaching it? Sometimes parents unintentionally teach their children neither what they want to teach them nor what they believe they are teaching them.

Regardless of the methods you are using at bedtime, your child is being taught *something*. Kelly and Tiffany, who would continually give into their children's nighttime demands, were actually teaching their children to make a huge fuss during the night.

Something similar was happening with Laura and James' son, Chip. His parents' "battle at bedtime" was giving him power in a troubling way. When parents are not in agreement about bedtime rules, the child is almost compelled to play them off against each other and see if he can get more time, more attention, more cuddling—and less alone time in his dark, scary room. In Chip's case, his parents are teaching him to continue to cry and be upset; at least some of the time, his mother will come in and hold him until he falls asleep.

In Amanda's case, circumstances initially required vigilance due to her child's illness. Once Merri's health became less of a concern, however, she was never helped to adjust to spending nights safely in her own bed. After a severely ill child returns to good health, continued sharing of the bed has more to do with the parent's anxiety than with the child's safety.

Am I Safe or Not?

When a child continues to be under the watchful eye of the parent at bedtime, he begins to believe that either he is not capable of taking care of himself or that he really is in some kind of danger in his room.

Stephanie, LICSW

After all, if his room is safe and he is capable of sleeping in it without something bad happening to him, then why isn't he? Of course, a child doesn't actually ask himself this question, but he is getting the message loud and clear.

No matter what the intention, we need to be careful that the message we are sending our child is the message we intend to send. When children are helped to sleep in their own beds, they develop a sense of self-confidence, self-care, and greater calmness.

The Stopper of the Unexpected

Bill and Lexie's Story: Twin Troubles

Bill and Lexie are both successful professionals on the fast track to top level management. Everything in their lives had been planned, including when they would have their first child, how long Lexie would stay out of work, and which daycare they would use. They planned to have a natural childbirth, Lexie would breastfeed for the first year or so, Bill would take paternity leave for three weeks, and their lives would just continue to be the well-oiled machine they had always been.

Fairly late in the pregnancy, Bill and Lexie discovered that they were to be the parents of twins. Before they had had time to adjust to that unexpected news, Lexie had to have the babies delivered by Caesarian section. Both babies were small but fully developed and healthy.

Because she hadn't been able to undergo a natural child-birth, Lexie was more determined than ever to nurse her babies. The experience was quite different from what she had envisioned! In trying to breastfeed two babies, her nipples were constantly sore and the process was painful. Instead of the blissful, nurturing experience she had expected, Lexie found nursing to be a torturous nightmare, during which she was usually crying. When the twins were 5 weeks old, Lexie developed mastitis in both breasts and had to abruptly stop breastfeeding.

She felt like a complete failure as a mother, and the post-partum depression she had been fighting, bloomed. Bill felt helpless: his wife was a weeping, exhausted wreck; someone was always crying, and he was sleep deprived and had to return to work. You can imagine the cycle of fear, guilt, and blame that developed here.

Lexie returned to work part time when the twins (Olivia and Jayden) were 8 months old. The twins were put into day-care. When she was at work, all Lexie could think about was her babies and what she wasn't doing for them; when she was home, she couldn't completely enjoy them, because all she could think about was how much work was piling up in her absence.

"I try to give each of them quality time; I want them to feel special. I know how important that is. I've read all the books, and I don't want them to be 'the twins;' I want them to feel like individuals, important because of WHO they are, not WHAT they are. But having two children the same age makes it so difficult. I never feel like I give enough of any-thing—time, attention, cuddling. I couldn't even give them enough of the one thing only I could provide—my breast milk. I love them so much, but I'm afraid they don't know it. I'm *really* afraid that they're going to resent me when they're older. I feel like a failure!"

Lexie, Bill, Olivia, and Jayden came for their initial con-sultation when the children were 4 years old. Essentially, neither Bill nor Lexie had had a full eight hours of sleep for four years. The twins had formed a successful alliance to ensure that they kept their parents busy until the wee hours of the morning. The kids got to nap at daycare; their parents just got more tired, more discouraged, more irritable.

"We used to talk about having four children," Bill told me; "we can't even manage two! Hell—we don't even have the time to *make* another kid!"

"Amen!" Lexie agreed.

The Stopper of History

Mickey and Jenn's Story: The Dreadful Day

When Mickey called for an appointment, he asked if he and his wife could be seen immediately, explaining that they were in crisis. Fortunately, I was able to see them that eve-ning. Jenn was a mess. She was crying in the waiting room and had obviously been crying for hours. Mickey was trying to comfort her, but he looked stricken.

As soon as the office door shut, Jenn blurted, "I'm a child abuser. I slapped my child—right across the face. I'm a pediatrician, for God's sake. How could I do that? My poor baby. She'll never forgive me. And my husband…I'm so sorry, Mickey. I wouldn't blame you if you wanted to divorce me."

Jenn and Mickey were the parents of two children, Josh, 4, and Pamela, 7. Jenn was a pediatrician at a neighborhood clinic catering to low-income families; Mickey was a contractor and a town councilman. Because of their jobs, both parents worked long hours, and frequently one or both of them got home late. The housekeeper, an older woman with grown children, would feed the children and stay with them until the parents came home, when necessary.

Starting with Pamela's birth, Jenn and Mickey arranged their schedules so that one of them was usually home with the baby. They also tried to make certain that their daughter got to spend some time with each of them every day, which might mean staying up late, being woken up and brought into the parent's bed, or being woken up early to have some time with Mommy or Daddy before she or he went off to work.

When there was just one child that system seemed to work well, and Pam showed no ill effects from her unusual, but benign schedule. In all other ways, her life was normal and well controlled. All that changed when Josh was born. With one child, a family can tolerate a certain amount of inconsistency. With more than one, an erratic schedule can move from relative disorganization to chaos, seemingly with the speed of light.

Bedtime became an issue with Pam for the first time, and she became whiny, stubborn, and rebellious. Mickey thought it was funny; Jenn wrote it off to the "temper tantrum three's." Eventually, Pam settled into a pattern of staying in her room most nights, after a rather prolonged getting-ready-for-bed procedure.

When Josh was ready, at age 3, to move into a bed, however, neither child wanted to stay in their rooms or abide by any schedule their parents decided to impose. Jenn and Mickey were totally unprepared for night after night of tantrums, crying, and children coming into their room at all hours. They found themselves unable to sleep and becoming irritable and short-tempered with the children.

Josh would have full blown tantrums at bedtime, which could last for hours. Pam started most evenings by refusing to eat her dinner and being sent from the table. It went downhill from there. Refusal to bathe, refusal to stay in her room, crying, going into Josh's room and waking him up—all were strategies that Pam now employed to delay bedtime.

Mickey's father had been a police chief and a firm believer in corporal punishment. Mickey was brought up to say "Yes, sir" to his father and not question any command. Over the bed in his childhood room hung a plaque inscribed, "You do the crime, you serve the time."

"My dad was full of these little slogans," Mickey commented. "There was the one over my bed, and then, 'Do the deed and you will bleed' or 'Talk back, and receive a crack'—that was an understatement, though. My dad backhanded me so hard once he knocked me out."

Mickey vowed that, under no circumstances, would he ever hit his children.

Jenn was brought up quite differently; her parents would threaten punishments—time-outs, grounding, loss of privileges—and then would never follow through. Jenn knew of her husband's upbringing and she knew that he had vowed never to act like his father. As a pediatrician, she also knew about generational family violence, and she was becoming nervous about his ability to remain calm in the face of such miserable behavior from their children.

She had noticed that lately Mickey had begun saying things like, "Do it again, your head will spin!" Although he said them in a joking manner, they were a bit too reminiscent of his father for Jenn's comfort.

On "The Dreadful Day," as they came to call it, both parents were exhausted from lack of sleep but had made a special effort to get home early and have a "family night." Jenn knew that bedtime had become a horror show, so she and Mickey strategized that maybe if they made a special night for the kids they could get their family back on track.

Mickey had made his kids' favorite spaghetti sauce—from scratch—and served it over shells. Jenn had bought a children's DVD just released that week. No sooner had they sat down to eat, when Pamela took one look at the pasta and said, "Ugh! That looks disgusting! It looks like puke!" Mickey turned white, and Jenn slapped her across the face.

Jenn was weeping as she recounted the incident. "I was worried about Mickey—how much he could stand. No sleep, job stress, and bratty kids. I didn't want him to ever hit one of them. I knew it would kill him. But he never did—I was the one."

The Biggest Stoppers: Guilt and Shame

Kelly and Tiffany, Laura and Chip, Bill and Lexie, and Mickey and Jenn are all capable adults who looked forward to having children, and had a pretty good idea of how they wanted to raise those children. Yet, all the planning, education, and good intentions in the world are no guarantee that serious problems will not arise.

Mickey and Jenn

Jenn loved her husband; she respected the kind of father he had chosen to be—especially after the example his own father had set. The act of slapping her daughter on "The Dreadful Day" was exactly *because* of her love and concern for Mickey. She was so involved in *protecting* him from doing something he would find unforgivable, that she did it herself. Overcoming her own guilt was the biggest challenge for Jenn.

As for Pamela—the injured party: she was bothered more by her mother's upset than by the slap itself. In spite of her mother's repeated assurances that Jenn was wrong and that there was no excuse for her to have slapped Pamela, Pamela felt guilty about being the cause of her mother's distress.

Mickey knew that the whole thing was his fault; if his wife hadn't been so worried about him, none of it would have happened. If he had been a better father, if had *had* a better father—if only. He was filled with shame and guilt that his wife was suffering because of who he was.

Josh was oblivious to the whole thing; he liked his dinner, watched the video, and was glad that his sister was "in trouble." No guilt there!

Bill and Lexie

"I feel so guilty and ashamed," were almost the first words out of Lexie's mouth when I met her. "I have a loving husband, a great job—well, right now it's awful, but I usually love it—and beautiful children. Money isn't a problem. Why can't I handle two kids? I just don't seem to be able to do anything well any more."

She and Bill were exhausted by the stress of managing two willful children and two demanding bosses—at the same time. She felt "globally inadequate," to use her phrase, and Bill felt as if he should be able to be of more help. Unfortunately, between trying to appease a difficult client in Hong Kong—who insisted on 4:00 A.M. telephone conferences—and getting to bed late because of Olivia and Jayden's antics, Bill was burned out.

"I feel guilty and ashamed for feeling guilty and ashamed!" Lexie said, through tears. "What's wrong with me?"

Laura and James

"Some days I think that Laura and Chip would've been better off if I'd re-upped," James declared. "I've made my wife feel like a failure, and my son is happier when I'm not around."

Kelly and Tiffany

"If we had realized what we were doing, we wouldn't have done it!" said Tiffany, referring to their policy of appeasement with the boys. "They seemed so little and needy, and we didn't want to be bad parents. So, we just kept giving in, giving in. Now, I not only feel like a bad parent, I feel like an incompetent idiot! My kids are just—awful! They behave so badly—and I made them that way. I'm so tired of feeling embarrassed by my own children."

Starter:
Understand What's Going On, and Be a Partner with Your Partner!

Fear, guilt, blame, anger, and self-doubt are very common when parents are having issues concerning bedtime. Unless the couple is absolutely on the same page about their child's evening routine and stick to it *no matter what*, problems will usually arise.

Initially, parents make excuses for the lack of good behavior at bedtime (e.g., it's not that bad, all kids get scared of being alone, she's just high-spirited, we don't mind when Harley comes into our bed—every night, he's just adjusting to the change in schools/routine/house/Grandma's presence-absence/whatever.) The couple knows that these are just excuses but are now caught up in justifying their own behavior—regardless of the initial causes. Kelly and Tiffany's experience with "The Weekend Away" earlier in this chapter is a prime example.

Then, it becomes a matter of "he said—she said" with each partner alternately blaming the other and then themselves for the problems. Laura blamed James for being too hard on Chip—but secretly knew it was her fault for babying him. James blamed Laura for her lack of structure and rules but knew it was really his inability to be flexible and open that was causing the problems.

Ultimately, the shame and guilt act as stoppers for each parent: they become so tired out—literally and figuratively—that they don't trust themselves to set up sensible rules and then stick to them. Even if they could figure out what to do, they doubt their own judgment. Kelly and Tiffany, Mickey and Jenn, James and Laura, and Lexie and Bill became paralyzed by their feelings of inadequacy—but not permanently.

Every one of these couples decided to partner *with their partner.* They came to recognize that their greatest strength was their love for each other and for their children. As the first step in bringing order to their lives, they made up their minds to act as a unit and to commit to the What's the Rule? technique.

Starter:
History Belongs in a Book— on a Shelf!

Dr. Pressman

This cycle of fear, guilt, recriminations, and self-doubt can seriously undermine a marriage. The only hard and fast truth we know about successfully raising children is that the central unit—the parents—must be solid. If they present a united front, the kids will prosper. If they are at odds, the kids will suffer.

Nowhere is that more apparent than at bedtime. When parents make up their minds to act as one in starting a bedtime routine, the children will benefit. They will feel safe and confident, and they will know that they can trust their parents to keep them safe. That's a winning combination.

Take all the old fears, the sack of guilt, and the list of blame you have developed, and label it "old stuff." Starting now, that's all ancient history. You're wiping the slate clean and starting something new—and that "something new" is going to make horrendous night times a distant memory.

I am happy to report that all four of the families we discussed previously are doing well. They deserve it; they worked hard at being good parents, and it wasn't always easy.

Conclusion

Every parent we have described is a good parent. Ever parent we have ever known—including ourselves—has made choices we wish we hadn't. But, as we said earlier—we have never met a perfect parent.

As parents, we face challenges with our children every day. Some days are just glorious; if there were any rough spots, they were so minor we don't even remember them. And then there are "The Dreadful Days;" those are the ones we wish we could forget, but can't.

Bedtime—nighttime—the whole ritual that starts with dinner/supper and progresses through the evening until the last person falls asleep: this is the time when the most difficult challenges arise. If a parent is going to have a "Dreadful Day," this is when it is most likely to occur.

Now you've met another group of good parents—and been introduced to quite a few kids, too. You have probably had at least one, "Oh my!" experience while reading—because the likelihood of seeing yourself, your spouse, or your child within these pages is high.

In Part Two, you were introduced to the system called What's the Rule? In Part Three, you learned about different personality types. Now, in Part Four, you will see how a number of families use this technique to solve their bedtime conflicts. Remember, What's the Rule? has been tested by thousands of parents, and it's calling your name.

OBSTACLES,
Achievements
AND Your
QUESTIONS

CHAPTER TEN

Obstacles and Achievements

The Mommy's Perspective

Parenthood:
It's a Lot Easier on Television!

Mommy Rebecca

Is it just me, or is being a parent harder than it used to be? When I was growing up, the biggest parental fears were teen pregnancy and STDs. Now we fear fatal super-viruses and school shootings. We hear all about peanut allergies, pedophiles, instant messaging, and social networking (both of which can be abused and cause terrible damage, even suicide, in kids). It seems as if there really *are* more things to be afraid of today.

When I think about it, though, I guess my parents faced some scary things, too. Maybe it feels harder because now I'm the parent. I'm the one with the responsibility; it's all on me. That's scary.

Good Parents—
Serious Problems

Stephanie, LICSW

This chapter is devoted to good parent stories. You have already met quite a few good parents and probably have identified with some—if not all—of them. These stories, culled from the hundreds of stories we have heard, each represent a specific type of family, with differing personalities, belief systems, life experiences, and habits. Therefore, each story presents its own specific set of challenges in starting What's the Rule?

Richard and Angela's Story: This Time It's Personal!

Issues:
Sympathetic/Vicarious Personality Type, Older Parent

Richard is a successful financial analyst. Always an over-achiever and Type A personality, he was immersed in building his career until he met Angela, when he had just turned 45. It was, as a matter of fact, at his 45th birthday party that his sister, an elementary school principal, introduced him to Angela, her new assistant. Despite the difference in their ages—Angela was 29—it was love at first sight. They were married six months later, and Jacob was born a week before their first wedding anniversary.

Having spent his childhood concentrating on excelling in school and his adult life immersed in his work, Richard was determined not to miss out on any part of Jacob's development. When Jacob was a baby, Richard worked from home so he could be his son's primary caregiver and Angela could continue in her career.

This pattern continued, so that it was Richard his son cried for when he had a bad dream, Richard who took him to play group, Richard who was there for every soccer practice, every baseball game. Richard was reliving the childhood he never had through Jacob.

When Angela and Richard came in for therapy, it was at Angela's insistence. She expressed concern about Richard's over-involvement in their son's life.

Angela: I called you because I was so upset. It's probably not that big a deal, but I think that Jacob—he's our 7 year old—is having problems. Richard was at a two-day conference last week, so I was the one to take Jacob to his baseball game. Jacob was sitting on the bench for most of the game, and I was aware that he kept watching me—looking worried.

At one point he ran over to me and told me not to worry, that he was fine with not playing. I thought that was a little weird—why would I worry? He went in for the last two innings in the outfield, and he missed catching a ball. The look on his face just broke my heart! Now keep in mind, Dr. Pressman, this is a bunch of 7 year olds playing baseball; they *all* miss catches, drop balls, can't hit, fall down. Honestly—it's hilarious!

But there's poor Jacob, looking like it's the end of the world that he didn't catch a ball. In the car going home, the poor kid is sobbing. I kept asking him why he was so upset. First, he said, "I don't want to play anymore." I told him he didn't have to, of course, but I thought he'd miss being with his friends. It seemed like he really had fun and looked forward to the practices.

After we got home, I finally got him to talk to me. He said that he didn't want to disappoint me, and he didn't want me to be mad at his coach!

Whose Game Is It?

As the story evolved, it turned out that Richard had gotten angry at the coach on numerous occasions; he thought that Jacob should have more playing time. As the youngest on the team, Jacob did play less than older players; that was the league policy. Richard did not agree with the policy.

When Jacob didn't get a hit or missed a catch, it would bother Richard more that it bothered Jacob. Jacob didn't expect to be a star in his first year of baseball, but the obvious pain suffered by his father made Jacob hypersensitive to his mistakes on the field.

It was the same with school, Angela reported. Richard was constantly having teacher conferences to ensure that Jacob was getting the most out of his first-grade experience. "It's a miracle that Miss Weburn doesn't hate Jacob!" Angela exclaimed. "Fortunately, she likes me—and she's got a good sense of humor. He may not always be so lucky."

The real problem, according to Angela, was that Richard allowed Jacob to sleep with them. This had become an almost nightly occurrence. Angela didn't sleep well, as Jacob kicked in his sleep.

> **Angela:** Many nights I end up on the couch in the den. It's ridiculous! I'm sure it's just a habit, now, for Jacob. I don't really think he's scared of the dark—or of his room—or much of anything. Or—if he is—it's because Richard has made him that way. It's not Jacob who needs the reassurance of our presence at night; it's Richard who needs to be with Jacob. I swear—if he could climb into Jacob's skin—inhabit Jacob's body—he would!

> **Richard:** I just want him to feel secure, to know that we're there for him. I can't stand for him to be afraid or in pain.

> **Angela:** Being there for him is not the same as living his life for him, Richard. And kids do get scared. They do experience pain. We learn to be adults by learning that we can survive fear and pain—not by being prevented from having it, or by always having someone there to make it better.

It Starts with Bedtime

Every time Angela tried to start a bedtime routine that focused on getting Jacob to stay in his room, Richard sabotaged it. When Jacob had a hard time doing something, Richard "helped" him.

Eventually, Richard came to understand that his son needed the opportunity to fail, to make mistakes, even to experience fear, in order to learn that he could manage and succeed—all by himself—in overcoming problems. He and Angela agreed to institute a bedtime routine, employing What's the Rule? It worked.

Jessica and Eric's Story: Too Torn to Parent Effectively

Issues: Guilty/Indulgent Personality Type, Separation Anxiety, Return to Work

Emma, first introduced in Chapter Two, is the 2 year old who would cry inconsolably when her mother left her to go to work. She would cry so hard that she would throw up. Was her mother leaving this little girl with an abusive monster? Hardly. Emma's daycare provider had an undergraduate degree in early childhood education and was the mother of three school age children. She cared for four preschool age children in her bright, cheerful, and immaculate home, which looked like a child's dream house. Every child had his or her own room for naps, and the daycare provider planned imaginative outdoor and indoor activities for the children. The kids adored her.

Emma was the daughter of Jessica and Eric. When they planned their married lives, it was always Jessica's intention to be a stay-at-home mom, a decision Eric supported. As a CPA (Certified Public Accountant) and auditor for the state, Jessica worked long hours and traveled frequently. She was looking forward to spending every minute with her firstborn, Emma.

Her husband, Eric, was an engineer; with two of his friends, they got the financial backing to form their own company.

As with many new businesses, however, the financial backing was inadequate, and Jessica felt forced to step in and work as an administrator so that Eric could go on the road.

In addition to being a conflicted working mother, Jessica also felt a tremendous amount of responsibility to keep her husband's fledgling company solvent. She worked tirelessly, pinching every corporate penny. She was well aware that the company could not afford to pay someone to do her job and that another employee would probably not be as dedicated.

Jessica always felt guilty: if she was at work, she was worried about Emma and the fact that someone else was raising her child four days a week; if she was with Emma, she was worried that she had left something undone at the office and that her oversight might damage the company.

Because Eric's travel schedule left Jessica and Emma home alone for three weeks out of every four, Jessica tried to be both supermom/dad for Emma. She indulged Emma's every wish, at the cost of her own need for adult companionship, downtime, and sleep. When Eric was away, Jessica allowed Emma to sleep with her. When Eric came home, Emma would cry so hard that she would end up in their bed. Emma's separation anxiety reached the point that Jessica couldn't even use the toilet without leaving the bathroom door open so that Emma could see her.

Eric, as much as he needed private time with his wife, also gave in to Emma's demands, rationalizing that he was gone so much, the least he could do was make his baby happy when he was there.

Jessica finally called for an appointment when Emma's daycare provider recommended it to her, saying that Emma's separation anxiety was detrimental to Emma and upsetting to the other children. When Jessica told Eric, he cancelled his forthcoming trip, stating "if the company succeeds but the family falls apart, what good is it?"

Within a few sessions, Eric had managed to restructure his schedule to share travel with his partners, who—though initially reluctant—discovered that their presentation and "people skills" were not as lacking as they had feared. Now traveling approximately one week out of every three, Eric was able to participate more in parenting, relieving Jessica of some of her responsibilities. They embraced the concept of What's the Rule? and were able to successfully implement it.

After the second week of sleeping in her own room, Emma was able to wave good-bye to her mother with only a request for one extra hug. Needless to say, the daycare provider was very pleased.

Ashley and Bobby's Story: The Dirty Little Secret

Issues: Away from Home, Problem Neighborhood, Social Isolation

Ethan, 10, was first introduced in Chapter Two. His parents, Ashley and Bobby, worked in retail. They lived in the town where they grew up, and both were heavily involved in their church. Ashley had never locked a door to either her house or her car, and she spoke with her mother every day. They had a good social life with other young parents, most of whom they had known since childhood. Bobby still enjoyed his nights out with the boys, and Ashley loved her girls' night out; she could shoot darts and whiskey with the best of them. They had managed their schedules so that one of them was always home with Ethan, and his life in their small town rental house was very safe and predictable.

Shortly before Ethan's fourth birthday, his parents decided that Bobby should go to graduate school and get his master of business administration degree (MBA). Ashley was nervous about moving away; she had never traveled more than a hundred miles from her home. Nonetheless, she was relieved that Bobby had finally settled on a career plan. When he was accepted into an MBA program, they were thrilled. They knew that it would be difficult both financially and personally, because it entailed a major move to a big city. However, they both believed that it would pay off in the long run.

Seemingly overnight, Ethan went from living in a neighborhood with lots of green grass to a third floor walk-up apartment in a dingy building. The neighborhood was mixed use—both residential and commercial—so it was not an ideal place for a family with a young child. Down the street was an X-rated video store, a popular gathering place for homeless people, drug dealers, and prostitutes.

Ashley had been unable to find affordable, quality daycare; it made more financial sense for her to stay home with Ethan. Unfortunately, there was little for them to do that was both inexpensive and safe. Ashley's daily calls home became increasingly tearful.

Understandably, both Ashley and Bobby became fearful parents. Raised in a small, friendly town, they were totally unprepared for life in an inner city. Ashley had her wallet stolen the first week when she paused to help an elderly woman. When a telephone repair man knocked on the door—there was a problem with some of the lines going into the building—Ashley became hysterical and called the police.

Nothing passes from a parent to a child faster than fear. No matter how hard Ashley and Bobby tried to convince Ethan that he was safe in their new home, their words were contradicted by their every gesture and look. By the time Bobby had successfully completed his master's degree, Ethan had become an extremely fearful child.

He delayed going to bed, using every strategy a bright child can employ. He would finally give in, only if a parent would stay in his room until he fell asleep. Unfortunately, his falling asleep did not mean that he stayed asleep. A light sleeper, he would wake up at the slightest noise. Then he would go into his parents' bed, and his parents, too wrung out from all the bedtime nonsense, would just pretend that he wasn't there.

The week before he graduated, Bobby was offered an excellent job managing the company of a family friend who was looking to retire. The company was 30 miles from Bobby's graduate school. Although not "back home," the location was a small town similar to the one they had left. They bought a house in a lovely area, joined the local church, and got settled in; the pattern of overprotection and fearfulness, however, was well-established.

Ethan would not go to play at a friend's house unless accompanied by a parent. If he was left at a friend's house— like for a birthday party—he would call continually with complaints until a parent came and either stayed with him or took him home.

At almost 10 years old, Ethan was still sleeping in his parents' bed and had never spent the night away from them. Interestingly enough, the straw that broke the camel's back (and brought Ashley and Bobby into therapy) was when Ashley was the only parent at a child's birthday party swinging a bat at the piñata. She was so used to doing what Ethan asked that she really didn't question his request for her to take his turn, because he was too scared. She suddenly registered the looks of surprise and shock on the faces of the other boys and the birthday boy's parents. Totally humiliated, she went home and called her pediatrician. She was mortified when Ethan's doctor suggested that she call Dr. Pressman, a child psychologist.

The first appointment was a relief for Bobby and Ashley. They felt as if their treatment of Ethan was a dirty little secret—that no one could possibly understand how they came to have a 10-year-old boy still sleeping in their bed. They felt acute embarrassment at Ethan's arrested psychological development, anger at themselves for promoting it, and anger at Ethan for not acting his age. Just talking openly about their problem and being treated with kindness and understanding—instead of the disapproval and disgust they were anticipating—was a very freeing experience. It took surprisingly little time for them to put What's the Rule? into practice, and for Ethan to take a huge jump into age-appropriate social interaction.

Missy and Christopher's Story: On One Thing, We Agree

Issues:
Divorce, Different Parenting Styles

Missy and Christopher are the divorced parents of Nicholas, age 7, and Sophia, age 3. A year after their divorce was final, they came in as a couple on the advice of the children's pediatrician.

Missy, who grew up in a working class family, was initially attracted to Chris's intelligence and ambition. Although he wasn't raised in a high-income home, Chris had two college-educated parents who stressed the value of education and hard work. Chris had decided on his career path by the time he was 16, and he never deviated from that path. When he and Missy met, he was starting a residency in general surgery, and she was an emergency room nurse. Chris was attracted by Missy's warmth and ability to connect with people; one of the things that made her such an excellent ER nurse was that she was able to reassure and calm patients so that it was easier for the doctors to work on them.

After 10 years of marriage and two children, Missy was sick of Chris's "aloof and superior" attitude, stating "He treats me like a scrub nurse—and he is totally condescending to his scrub nurses!"

Chris felt that Missy's parenting "lacks direction—our kids are all over the place."

Missy: He thinks they should already be prepping for their SAT's—or LSAT's—or MCAT's, for Christ's sake. They're kids, not little success machines!

Chris: Children need structure and direction. I provide that; Missy doesn't.

And so it went. The one thing that Missy and Chris agreed on was that their differences were having a negative effect on their children. They were both devoted parents and wanted the shared custody arrangement to work. As it was, the children were having transition problems moving between households, because their parents' expectations and rules were different. Therefore, there was a period of "testing behavior" from the children during exit and entry of each residence, which was tedious for their parents. Bedtime, of course, was the focal point of tension in both homes.

Missy: I feel like they are so needy when they get back from Chris's that I have a hard time actually getting them into bed. I don't mean that they are abused or anything, it's just that he's a lot stricter than I am, so I guess I try to compensate—too much.

Chris: I feel like the bad cop! I put Sophia to bed, leave the room, and she starts to cry. Then I see Nick getting more and more anxious until it's time to go to bed, when he starts to cry and asks to call his mom. Nights are rough.

Missy: Actually, we agree on that.

Both Missy and Chris wanted Nick and Sophia to have good and happy memories of their childhood; both were concerned that, if things didn't improve, their children's memories would be of unremitting stress. When the concept of What's the Rule? was introduced, Chris immediately saw the logic and was ready to put it into play that night. Missy was more cautious; she wanted to plan it out and then have a family meeting to discuss their joint decision with the children.

Missy's "family meeting" took place in my office, after the couple had two more planning sessions with me. (Please see Chapter Eleven: Just the FAQ's, Page 147.) Both parents explained the What's the Rule? technique to the children, with each parent explaining exactly how that would translate to the bedtime routine in his or her own house (i.e., baths vs. showers, etc.). Because the parents were on the same page, the technique was established successfully in both households.

The children's reaction to the family meeting and the implementation of the technique was interesting. Chris commented that Nicholas and Sophia were obviously pleased and relieved to see their parents united and acting together. Evidently, even if going along with What's the Rule? meant giving up some of their power at bedtime, it was a small price for the children to pay for the security of having consistent rules in both households. Both Missy and Chris reported that there was virtually no testing behavior at bedtime in either of their homes.

Brandon and Heather's Story: Good Pal Does NOT Equal Good Parent

Issues: Divorce, ADHD, Food Sensitivity, Life Style Differences

Brandon and Heather are the divorced parents of Tyler, age 4. Heather is a freelance media consultant. Although being "on call" for her clients can be from early morning until late at night, Heather has organized her life around her son; her assistant manages all but the most severe crises that occur outside of conventional business hours. Heather has promised Tyler that she will be there for his "special things," and has a large calendar posted on the kitchen wall that has all of Tyler's play dates, nursery school events, soccer practices, music lessons, and other activities clearly marked. Heather has also supplied Tyler's father with a copy of his schedule, so he always has the option of attending activities.

Heather is "hands-on" mother who tries to keep Tyler's life as calm and organized as she can. When something interferes with her attendance at one of Tyler's events, she makes certain that he knows ahead of time, that he understands the reason, and that there is another activity (e.g., "pizza night") that occurs as soon after the missed event as is practical. Heather wants Tyler to grow up feeling that his world is a safe, predictable place.

Brandon is a fireman with a large, municipal fire department. Much of the time, his hours are regular and his schedule predictable. Because of seniority, Brandon now has most weekends off, and Tyler stays with him during that time. Brandon is a self-confessed "excitement junkie."

> **Brandon:** I don't want Ty to be afraid to try new things. I want him to be spontaneous, you know, the whole *carpe diem* thing. When an opportunity comes along, I grab it; I want Ty to be the same.

> **Heather:** Spontaneity is fine; I'm spontaneous—within reason. But children need consistency, Brandon. At my house, Tyler has a schedule. It suits him. He has his dinner at 5:30, his bath—which can be really long—at 6:00. Then we read books, maybe watch one of his videos, and he's in his bed by 7:30. And he crashes—he's tired by then. Sometimes, depending on the day, he's asleep

by 7:00. This kid needs about 12 hours of sleep, or he's a really unhappy camper. When I get him back from you on Sunday—whenever that is!—he's exhausted, cranky, defiant, and miserable. He doesn't want to obey any rules, he won't stay in his room, he always has at least one tantrum, he cries himself to sleep, and he has a tough day at nursery school on Monday. Monday night is hell, too. By Tuesday, I have him back on track. Then Friday, he goes to you—and the routine is totally shot.

Brandon: Come on, Heather. I ask him if he wants to go to bed, and he gets really sad. So, I let him stay up and spend time with his dad. And—sometimes—I let him sleep with me. Why not? You make it sound like I'm taking the kid to strip joints, or something!

Heather: Are you? I didn't mean that. Look, I know that you love Tyler a lot. I just don't think you're a very good…

Brandon: Father? Go ahead. I know that's what you think; you might as well just tell the doctor everything. I was a lousy husband, and now I'm a lousy father. I'm not always on time. I change my plans. I don't conform to your "schedules." Look, Doc, you don't know what it was like being married to such a control freak. She should be on medication or something!

Heather: You're such an ass!

Brandon: Says you! But I am a good Dad, and you're not going to take my son away from me.

Their mutual love for their son was the *only* thing Heather and Brandon had in common. Brandon loved his bachelor life. In an individual session, he admitted that he probably should never have gotten married and that he had cheated on Heather. College life, fraternity parties, late nights, and lots of ladies were his idea of fun. He was a rule breaker, and he saw no reason why Tyler should have to conform to his mother's rules when in his father's home. He wanted to be "the cool Dad" for his son, and that meant staying up late, eating whatever was fun and easy, "going with the flow."

This created problems for both Tyler and Heather. Tyler was kept on a regulated diet—as free from sugar and food additives as possible—in an attempt to regulate his ADHD. He did better when the diet was maintained; when he had an influx of sugar, caffeine, or food additives (prepared or junk food), he experienced mood swings, attention problems, irritability, headaches, and sleep problems. Tyler also required more sleep than the usual 4 year old in order to function well.

Both parents and Tyler were well aware of Tyler's dietary constraints. Heather followed them, and Tyler did well. Brandon did not choose to comply with them and Tyler—a typical kid—was not going to refuse treats and his favorite junk foods when offered them by his dad. Brandon also did not observe regular bedtimes, preferring to have Tyler stay up and play video games with him. Therefore, by the time Tyler returned to Heather, he was truly a mess.

> **Heather:** I know that Brandon loves his son, but every time I say good-bye to Tyler on Friday, I feel like I'm sending my child off to be cared for by another child. It's not fair to Tyler and it's not fair to me. But what can I do? Tyler adores his daddy; I can't keep him from seeing him.

This, as you can imagine, was a very difficult situation. Heather once jokingly referred to their predicament as "The Case of the Worried Mom and the Weekend Warrior." For example, Brandon had taken Tyler to a professional football game, where Tyler had consumed two hot dogs, a bag of popcorn, cotton candy, and two sodas. When Brandon brought Tyler home to Heather's after the game, Tyler walked in the door and threw up all over the living room. Brandon's reaction was, "Whoops!"

Brandon loved his son; he wanted to be a good parent, and set a good example. His idea of parenting, however, was more on the order of fraternity buddies than father and son. Brandon and Heather were never going to be on the same page in terms of discipline and scheduling for Tyler; Brandon did come to understand, over time, that the example he was setting for his son was inappropriate and unhealthy. After they consulted with Tyler's pediatrician and got a list of dietary recommendations, we were able to work out a modified version of What's the Rule? for the time Tyler spent with his father.

Brandon agreed to have a "Tyler's Food" cupboard, which contained cereals, soups, and snacks that Tyler was allowed to eat. He also agreed to eliminate soft drinks entirely and keep fresh fruit and juices available.

Although Brandon was not willing to commit to a specific bedtime for his son, he promised that at his house the rule would be that Tyler would go to bed and sleep all night in his own room. He would return Tyler to his mother's house by 4:00 on Sunday. That gave Tyler and Heather some play time together to ease Ty's "re-entry" into a more structured environment, before the start of their evening routine.

One of the suggestions for a re-entry activity that would be both fun and relatively calm was cooking together. Heather and Tyler started planning a menu for Sunday nights that they could prepare together; things like meatballs and spaghetti are fun to make, and then children have a vested interest in eating them.

What's the Rule? was ultimately employed in both houses—not exactly as Heather would have liked it, but as an improvement over the previous situation. Tyler was calmer when he arrived home on Sundays, and sleep hygiene was able to be restored. As somebody once said, "You do the best you can with the cards you're dealt!"

The Mommy's Perspective

Mommy Rebecca

I have a stepchild. His name is Bobby and he is amazing. He always laughs when, on his birthday, I remind him how wonderful his delivery was and how he didn't give me a single stretch mark! I understand how complicated multiple household families can be. When there are two households in your child's life, you have to try and focus on what you can control in *your* house.

Heather chose to lead by example instead of playing the nagging ex-wife or the victim. She was successful in establishing some new guidelines with her ex-husband to try and lessen some of the dietary and sleep concerns. The modified version of What's the Rule? made her time with her child more enjoyable. Sometimes that's all you can do.

Stepping Very Carefully!

Stephanie, LICSW

Another situation that can provide real challenges is when you are dealing with a blended family—children from different marriages. Not only are there different houses with different rules, but there are often serious adult personality conflicts to overcome. When you are the birth parent, you may be concerned about your ex and his or her new spouse:

◆ Saying negative things about you

◆ Spoiling your child to gain favor and be the "fun parents" or

◆ Making your child the "Cinderella," or outsider, of the family.

If you are the stepparent, you may be dealing with some of the same concerns, plus other, equally difficult problems.

◆ Your stepchild says that you are not his REAL mom/dad; therefore, he doesn't have to do what you say.

◆ Your spouse is overly concerned with making sure his or her child feels wanted in your home, so your spouse spoils the child, making your life miserable.

◆ Your spouse doesn't want you to discipline his or her child—making your life miserable!

Danielle and Mike...and Sometimes Jason: Stepparent Misery

Issues:
Stepparenting, Blended Families

Danielle had always wanted to be a mother. She married her high school sweetheart right out of college and was divorced two years later. When Danielle was 25, she met Mike. He was the complete opposite of her first husband. He was an adult! It didn't take long for Danielle to fall in love with Mike. It didn't even bother her that Mike was 11 years older than she and had an 8-year-old son, Jason. After all, he had been divorced for six years. It was a messy divorce, and he and his ex-wife were barely on speaking terms by the time Danielle entered the picture. In fact, Mike only had custody of Jason every other weekend.

Danielle married Mike three years after meeting him in a small private ceremony held in their backyard. She and Mike planned to start trying to have babies right away— after all, she didn't want Mike to be 60 by the time she got pregnant! They conceived within months, and the birth of Brody— according to Danielle—is when everything changed.

Danielle: Jason and I were never *super* close, but things used to be okay, often really fun. Jason is a smart kid, and he's interested in some cool stuff. We used to have some good talks. When he came over he basically just preferred to hang out with Mike, which I understood. I mean, we would do things together, but it was obvious that he wanted his "dad time."

Lisa—that's Mike's ex-wife—is such an evil witch; I know she says horrible things about me to Jason, which sucks because I never do it to her! Even before we had Brody, she would pull crap with me like always—at the very last minute—changing the time we were to pick up Jason. Oh, that's another thing—we are always stuck driving! Even if *she* changes the plans, we have to drop everything and go pick him up. But God forbid that we should ever request a change of schedule. I mean, weeks ahead of time, like for my sister's wedding. You'd think we were asking for the moon!

After a few sessions, Danielle revealed that her feelings for Jason had changed since the birth of her biological child.

Danielle: [sobbing] I love Brody so much and I just want him to have a normal life. It would be so much easier if Jason just wasn't around. Oh my God, that sounds so terrible, but it's true. Sometimes I think, just six more years! In six more years he'll be 18 and I won't have to deal with this any more.

Mike: I know that Danielle loves Jason. She's really good to him, and he loves her, too.

Danielle: At least at Christmas and his birthday!

Mike: You know he loves you, honey. He just feels like if he gets close to you, he's being disloyal to his mother. Danielle's right about that, Dr. Pressman; my ex-wife is

vindictive, which is one of the reasons I divorced her—
one of the many reasons, actually. She does bad-mouth
Danielle and me. The difference is, I'm Jason's dad, and
he's not that crazy about his stepfather, so he's always
been close to me. Danielle is the "stepmonster;" I think
he actually likes her more than his mother, but Lisa's…
his mother.

Danielle: I know. And I do understand. But it hurts me,
Mike, that when Jason's around, you ignore Brody and
me. It's like we don't exist. I want Jason and Brody to
be close, but Jason is taking his cues from you. You act
like Brody isn't important to you, so that's what Jason
models.

As the story unfolded, the issue of Jason's bedtime came
up as a major problem. Mike was having his "bonding time"
with Jason at night, watching movies or attending sporting
events. This meant that Jason would often get to bed at 11:00
P.M. or later on both Friday and Saturday nights. He then
wanted to sleep-in the next morning, which made family
outings difficult. Brody and Danielle were up at 6:30 or 7:00 in
the morning and ready to go out and play by 9:00. Mike was
often just getting up at that time, and Jason was still asleep.
Usually, Danielle would end up taking Brody apple-picking,
or to the fair by herself—the kind of fun events she always
imagined doing with her baby and his daddy. Not alone.

The Dreadful Day
If Jason was awakened—like the day in October when the
family had planned a special day-trip—he was cranky, irritable, and rude to Danielle. That ended up being a "Dreadful
Day." Jason complained, put down everything they did as
"a waste of time," and refused to eat the beautiful lunch

Danielle had packed so they could picnic on the wharf; he was just wretched all day.

Danielle was angry and hurt, because she had worked hard to plan the outing. Mike was furious with his son and felt awful for his wife. Brody, sensitive to the tension, was unusually fussy. Jason knew he had successfully undermined his stepmother's "stupid trip;" he also knew that he had crossed the line with his father, who was obviously ripped. Jason sulked in the backseat listening to his Ipod all the way home, and he went to his room the minute they arrived. Danielle heard him on the phone to his mother but didn't listen. She just fed Brody and put him to bed, then retired to her room to cry. That night, holding his sobbing wife, Mike agreed that family therapy was in order.

The weekends with Jason had become a nightmare for Mike, too, as he was missing out on time with his wife and baby, and he felt he had "created a monster" in Jason. What's the Rule? became the solution for this family.

My House, My Rules

Mike and Danielle brought Jason with them for several sessions—which wasn't easy. Initially Lisa, Jason's mother, refused to allow him to be in counseling. It was only when Mike threatened to take her to back to court—and revisit the generous child support he was paying—that she agreed.

Jason was responsive to the family sessions. It was apparent that he was afraid of losing his father—and of completely alienating Danielle. He never said anything negative about his mother or his life at her home, but he volunteered that he enjoyed the kind of "family stuff" that Danielle planned. He liked the day trips and said that he wanted to be a more active "big brother" to Brody.

Surprisingly, Jason listed "Danielle's cooking" as one of the "Things I Enjoy" about staying at his father's house. This evolved into Danielle giving Jason cooking lessons, which was a Friday night or Saturday afternoon activity that they both enjoyed.

What's the Rule?—in bed by 10:00 P.M.—was the catalyst for all the positive changes that occurred in this household. The bedtime routine went like this:

1. Friday night: Cooking with Danielle or bathing and feeding Brody, dinner, game time with Danielle, Mike, and Jason. Shower, brush teeth, and in bed by 10:00.

2. Saturday night: Cooking and eating together and then whatever activities have been planned. Shower, brush teeth, and in bed by 10:00.

Mike, Danielle, Jason, and Brody are a happy family. Good rules—thoughtfully crafted—work.

Brooke and Matthew's Story: All Parented Out!

Issues: "Hands-On" Parenting, Overcommitment of Time, No Boundaries, Sibling Rivalry

When Brooke and Matthew started a family, they had already decided on their parenting strategy. They wanted to be "hands-on" parents and actively involved in their children's lives.

As a child, Brooke had no worries. She had no time to worry! Between sailing, swimming, and tennis lessons in the summer, and skiing, gymnastics, and ballet lessons in the winter, not to mention the various teams of which she was a member (soccer, basketball, softball), she was a busy little girl. She had lots of friends and enjoyed her active life. What she did not have was any one-on-one time with either of her parents. Although she had lots of memories of "doing things" as a child, she has no memories of special times with her mother or father. They were there, but they didn't really interact with either Brooke or her sister. Brooke decided that when she became a mother, her children were going to have a host of special memories of things they did with their mommy.

Matthew also had no memories of doing things with his parents. He, too, was very involved in sports from an early age. Holidays were spent with his parents' friends, summers he was at camp, and during the school year he saw very little of his parents. "They were always at work," according to Matthew. He remembers feeling sad when one of his friends would talk about going fishing with his father or spending time in the woodshop learning how to use the tools. "My parents worked very hard to give us a comfortable life. I think I would have preferred less comfort and more time with them."

When they came in for counseling, Brooke and Matthew were all parented out. Their kids—three boys, ages 3, 6, and 9—had worn them down.

"We've really messed up," Matthew stated. "When we had our kids, we wanted to be there with them—for them. It was important to us to have quality time with each kid, because Brooke and I didn't have that with our own parents.

"The problem is that we're so busy creating opportunities for them that we've turned into our parents, sort of. We're just so...busy!"

"We're not busy," said Brooke, "we're crazy! We're just running around frantic all the time. I feel exhausted; Matthew is beyond exhausted. He goes to an office all day and then barely has time to grab a bite before he's out the door to coach a team or lead a Cub Scout troop. I spend all day doing the house things—you wouldn't believe the laundry three active boys generate—and running Terry (the 3 year old) to play dates, as well as coming up with fun stuff for us to do together. Then the other two get home, and I'm the chauffer mom—the one who takes all the kids to practices, brings the snacks, and makes the arrangements—because the other mothers *work*.

"We help them with their homework, but it's downhill from then on."

When Harry, now 9, was a baby, Brooke and Matthew decided to try the family bed. During her pregnancy, Brooke had read some articles about the benefits of co-sleeping. The articles claimed that this method created early bonding with both parents, and contributed to feelings of safety and confidence in children. They thought it sounded good, so they started as soon as Harry was born. They enjoyed it, until he became a toddler and a very "active" sleeper. Still, they persevered, and when Max, now 6, was born, they tried to incorporate him. It didn't work.

At that point, Harry was almost 4 and was not going to give up his parents' bed. Adding insult to injury, Max suffered from asthma, so it seemed better to have him in a portacrib beside the master bed. Harry resented the special attention paid to Max, and Brooke and Matthew—determined to meet each child's needs—would alternate spending the night with him in his room. By the time Terry arrived, they were in deep trouble.

"It's a horror show every night," said Matthew. "If we manage to get Terry settled by 7:30 or so, then Max and Harry start up. They won't shower on time, and they fight over everything. We have a schedule posted, but they totally ignore it. Max still wants one of us in his room until he falls asleep, and if we don't, he has mega tantrums and gets Terry up.

"Harry keeps coming out of his room to watch TV with us, as if he's a grown-up. It's like he always wants to show his brothers that he's 'the man!' When we send him back to his room, he makes so much noise that, if the other kids *happen* to have fallen asleep, he wakes them up.

"Every night it's the same thing—we rarely get to sleep before midnight, and we have to get up by 6:00. Of course, just because we actually get to sleep doesn't mean we'll stay asleep. At least four nights a week, one of them comes into bed with us—sometimes they all end up in there. And honestly, we're just too tired to throw them out. I'm at a loss, Doc," Matthew said.

Brooke wrings her hands. "People say to me, 'You're so lucky you can afford to stay home with your kids.' Please! I would so much rather work; it's a lot easier. It's embarrassing to admit this, but I'm desperate, Dr. Pressman. I know you've probably heard it all, but we've created monsters. I don't even *like* them a lot of the time! What kind of mother says that about her own kids?"

Loving and Liking Are Two Different Things

What kinds of parents say that they've created monsters? Good mothers say that and so do good fathers. More good parents think it—frequently. We can love our children dearly but find them periodically quite unlikable—and find their behavior downright horrid!

Stephanie, LICSW

By concentrating so much on having a parenting model different from what they had experienced as children, Brooke and Matthew lost sight of the goal: a healthy, happy family. They mistook frenetic involvement for nurturing. The children were running the house, and no one was enjoying it.

The first step in creating a family plan that worked for everyone was the development of a realistic bedtime routine.

Using much the same model as the one Liz and Ben used in Chapter Seven, Brooke and Matthew looked at the kids' schedules and their own availability. They came up with doable bedtime timetables for each boy, then scheduled both the *time* of the family meeting and the *approach they would take* when presenting What's the Rule?

Using "How old are you now?" they were able to explain the new bedtime rules with some humor. By the end of the meeting, each child could repeat the Rule as it applied to himself.

They presented the plan on a Sunday morning, and had a very pleasant, active day with the boys. They started What's the Rule? that night. It took five nights for the boys to adjust, but Brooke and Matthew were real troopers. They stuck to their plan, and on the sixth night, there were no problems. That was more than a year ago, and there have been only good nights since then.

Once Brooke and Matthew put What's the Rule? into place, life became manageable. What a relief!

The Mommy's Perspective

As far as parenting is concerned, I understand how quickly days turn into weeks, and weeks turn into years. When my daughter was first born, people used to say to me, "Enjoy this time! They grow up so fast." I would respond politely, "I know."

Mommy Rebecca

Truthfully, I found this saying kind of annoying. Now, I understand it. It helps to explain how patterns are gradually formed. Time really does pass quickly, especially after having children! If I were handed a perfectly healthy 8-year-old child, I wouldn't even consider letting him or her sleep in my bed. As parents we get into these situations by degrees. Many parents—like Amanda—have had a circumstance that explains why their children are still in bed with them, or why nighttime is such a challenging time.

We all want to be good parents; we just don't always know the best way to do it. I know that among the parents of my children's friends, bedtime is the number one problem. (Homework, with school age kids, is the number two problem; that's another book.) It often seems like it's easier to ignore problems; but you and I both know, they don't go away just because we want them to. We need to solve them—permanently.

Conclusion

Every family we introduced in this book ultimately used the What's the Rule? technique to solve their bedtime challenges. None of the families we discussed came into therapy specifically because of bedtime breakdowns. Yet, the daytime problems for which they sought help were resolved when the nighttime problems were settled.

The *absence* of a structured bedtime routine will *not* cure Merri's chronic illness; it will *not* restore Jimmy's father to him; *nor* will it solve the sibling rivalry between Harry, Max, and Terry. It *will*, however, *create* serious problems for children and unhappiness for their parents.

This system is not too good to be true. You know that, for sure, after reading the blow-by-blow descriptions of establishing What's the Rule in two different households. What's the Rule? is not easy, but it is simple. Using *Matilda and Maxwell's Good Night* makes it even more user-friendly. Good Nights are within your grasp, good parent. Go get them!

Just in case you have a lingering question or two, check out the next and final chapter: Just the FAQ's!

CHAPTER ELEVEN

Just the FAQ's!

After giving a lecture or seminar about What's the Rule? parents inevitably have questions. Below are the ones most frequently asked, in question and answer format.

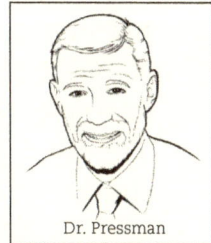

Dr. Pressman

Q: What is "the meeting," also known as "the family meeting"?

A: The meeting is when all the caregivers sit down with the child to introduce the new rule or to deal with an issue that has resulted from a new or an established rule. It is usually held in the morning. It occurs after all the caregivers are in agreement about the new rule. The tone of the meeting is kind and relaxed but assertive.

Q: What is "the gesture"?

A: It is a way of reinforcing the rule without words. After the rule is in place, when your child "forgets" the rule by getting out of bed or coming out of the bedroom, you ask, "What's the rule?" There will be only one of three responses: (1) He will shrug his shoulders, (2) he will introduce a red herring (e.g., "I hate your stupid rule!"), or (3) He will tell you, "The rule is 'In bed at 8:00 for the night.'" In the first two cases, you gently state "The rule is, 'In bed at 8:00 for the night'"... no more than this. In all three cases, follow with the gesture. You look toward the bed or bedroom. Then, with an open palm, point in that direction with eyebrows raised, signaling that you expect your child to go there.

Q: What happens if my child cannot remember the rule?

A: This is not a time to teach your child to remember the rule. The format is quite simple. If you are at the meeting, state the rule. Ask your child to repeat it so that you are both sure he has it right. If your child cannot remember or shrugs his shoulders, simply repeat the rule and leave it at that. If sometime after the meeting you ask, "What's the rule?" (for example, when he comes out of the bedroom after bedtime) and he cannot remember or shrugs his shoulders, state the rule but do not ask him to repeat it.

Q: Is it better to have bedroom doors opened or closed at night?

A: Some parents are rather insistent or at least more comfortable if everybody's bedroom door (including their own) is open during the night. Perhaps this starts during the first few weeks of the baby's life, when parents are particularly vigilant. However, a continued "open-door policy" usually presents problems; the least of which is that parents have less opportunity to do whatever they might want to do behind closed doors. It also conveys to many children that they will only be safe if the doors are open. Some parents may leave the doors open because they believe that their children will feel more secure. In fact, this leads their children to feel less secure.

The open-door policy also makes it more difficult to reinforce good bedtime behavior and does nothing to help your child gain self-confidence. It facilitates and almost welcomes children leaving their bedroom and walking into their parents' bedroom. Having doors closed will ultimately need to be a goal for the complete bedtime routine. In addition, closed doors greatly reduce the spread of fire, as any fire marshal will tell you.

Q: We've started to keep the bedroom door shut. What do we do when our child keeps knocking on it?

A: The first time, open your door and ask, "What's the rule?" Use the gesture, and then gently close the door. If she continues this behavior, ignore it for the night—no matter how long she persists. If the behavior goes on for an extended period, discuss it briefly at the meeting. Start over each night with the same routine—opening the door only on the first time. Never respond to your child through the closed door.

Q: Can't we wean our child into sleeping in his bed by lying with him until he falls asleep?

A: The message to your child is that you do not believe he can do it on his own. I've never seen this technique work, at least for any length of time. Most often when your child wakes up, he will be aware that you are gone and then seek you out.

Q: My child does not hear me when she is in front of the TV. What should I do?

A: There is an alien tractor beam that is sent out from the TV to capture your child's mind (well okay, the TV is more interesting than you are). To communicate, you must step between the TV and your child to break the beam. If she keeps moving her head or body to reestablish the beam, turn off the TV while you talk.

Q: Is it okay to leave a nightlight on in my child's room?

A: If your child is not playing or reading during the night because of the light, it seems okay. Sometimes, however, it will slow down development of nighttime independence. If nighttime fears continue after a week of starting the routine, it is time for the nightlight to go.

Q: We discovered that our daughter is sleeping next to our door. What should we do?

A: First use the meeting to explain what you are going to do to help your daughter follow the rule, which, in every case, includes the phrase "in bed by." When and if you get up and you are aware that your child is camped out next to your door, you turn on a light and ask, "What's the rule?" Her behavior is really no different than any other time a child leaves the bedroom after bedtime. If this behavior continues beyond three days, this time at the meeting, tell your child that you will be affixing a chime or bell on her door that will help remind her about "the rule" (and help you wake up to quickly reinforce it.) The learning curve won't be as long if you can ask "What's the rule?" as soon as possible upon your child leaving her bedroom.

Q: When should I carry my child back to his bedroom?

A: Picture yourself carrying a 185 pound football player back to bed while invoking this technique. Any carrying is the absolutely last resort and is reserved for children under the age of 3. The thought process of very young children is still a tad primitive and is much slower, if not completely shut down, when they are tired. Although older children will eventually leave your bedroom at night if you use the various forms of delivering "What's the Rule?" a 3 year old may just go to sleep on the floor next to your bed.

Any child older than 3, no matter where he is found sleeping outside of his bedroom, should be woken up and guided—but not carried—to bed. Your child will not learn how to take care of himself or to participate in What's the Rule? if he falls asleep in your bed or on the floor and miraculously wakes up in his bed the next morning.

Q: Our child crawls into bed with us. We don't notice this until we're ready to get up. What should we do?

A: It sounds like you have an open-door policy—see question above. Consider discarding this policy and shutting (if necessary, locking) your bedroom door at night.

If the problem occurs in the early stages of starting What's the Rule? immediately get out of bed and turn on the lights. Then go through the procedure—asking the question and using the gesture when appropriate. Wait for your child to leave, then shut your door and go back to bed.

Q: I'm divorced and my husband (or wife) doesn't have any clear rules about bedtime. What should I do?

A: Although you can try to come to an agreement with your ex-spouse, I've found only a handful of divorced or separated parents who can agree on a plan. If there was very little agreement about child raising prior to separation, the chance of agreement after separation is likely to be close to zero. However, there is no harm in trying. Give your spouse a copy of this book. If it is read, that is a positive sign. If it is not read or if it gets thrown away or "lost," read the next paragraph.

The somewhat good news is that unless there are very serious physical or psychological safety issues, such as abuse, sleepovers are usually more beneficial than detrimental. Similar to how children learn that there different rules for the playground and for the library, they also learn that rules are different at mom's and dad's houses. Your children can do just fine with using the technique at your house.

Q: My child stays up for hours in bed watching videos, playing Nintendo, texting, instant messaging, watching TV, etc. What should I do?

A: Add a "lights out" clause to the rule—that is, in bed for the night at 9:00, *lights out* at 9:30. Cell phones, iPods, gaming devices, TVs, computers, etc. need to be turned off and put in a designated place. For the first week or so, reinforce the rule by checking, and asking "What's the rule?" when necessary, possibly using the gesture toward the designated electronics storage place.

If the problem persists, have the meeting the following morning and explain that you expect the rule to be followed that night. Explain that the item will be removed the *following* night if there is a problem tonight. This is done only for one night at a time to "assist" your child in remembering. Never remove the item at the time of the offense. It is not an emergency. Removing the item the following morning will avoid a nighttime confrontation and will be more effective. I recommend removal of electronics only for *one night at a time* so that there is a constant opportunity for your child to demonstrate following the rule.

Q: What if my child stays up and plays with toys at night?

A: This problem is similar to the question above concerning the use of electronic equipment, except that your child is likely to be younger. At the meeting discuss the possibility of having toys put away in a container in your child's room just before bedtime.

Q: One night, we had a fire in our historic house that was caused by old wiring. Thankfully, the damage was limited. However, since then our daughter is terrified at night. What is the best thing to do?

A: From time to time, I've seen situations where there is an absolutely logical reason for a child to feel unsafe. This is extremely rare. However, safety issues must be resolved immediately. When reasonable safety is restored, in the meeting, be sure to once again (assuming that you have already done so) acknowledge the fear and concern of your child. Emphasize that you are absolutely sure that all is safe now, and that Mom and Dad feel 100% fine about her sleeping in her room. Reaffirm the bedtime rule. Add that you know she will be able to comfort herself, have a good experience in her bedroom, and start feeling really confident again. Then reinforce the rule, just as you did before.

Q: John, who is 8 years old, shares a bedroom with his younger brother Timmy, who is 4 years old. We're concerned that John's crying and tantrum behavior at bedtime will wake up Timmy. We also worry that Timmy will start to learn bad behavior from his older brother. What should we do?

A: This is a common and often stressful problem for parents. Actually there are two concerns. First, let's look at the one about the younger child learning bad behavior from the older child. What the 4 year old learns most is *how the parents* handle his older brother. He sees that their parents have clear rules that are kindly but consistently reinforced. He also sees his brother's behavior starting to change, which is a powerful lesson. Any disruption in Timmy's sleep will be over in a matter of days. Contrast this to the constant bad example when John was sleeping in his parents' bed.

Second, about John waking up Timmy: When John creates a fuss in his room, go into the room. If he is out of his bed, which is likely, you ask him, "What's the rule?" Other than repeating the rule, all the rest is done with no more words from you. You use the gesture. Chances are good that he will comply. You may have to wait patiently, even several minutes, which will seem like hours. Then leave. Repeat as necessary.

If Timmy complains, leave John in the room, and beckon Timmy to come with you out of the bedroom. Explain to Timmy what is happening, and that the family will meet tomorrow to discuss the problem; ask him to bear with it for now. In brief, calmly reinforce the rule with both children. Any attempt to admonish or side with a child will be the same as reacting to a red herring. At the meeting, acknowledge that last night was a difficult one. The children might chime in with complaints; however, just listen. Don't provide solutions; simply restate the rule and indicate that you hope everyone has a good night.

This entire strategy may need to be repeated for several nights. It is one of the more challenging problems we see. Take heart, it will work if you stay with it.

Q: What if my child is sick?

A: This is somewhat age dependent. In the case of a young child who, according to physicians, typically needs observation while they are sick, arrange for one of the caregivers in your household to be with your child *in your child's room*. It means that the caregiver may have to be up all night sitting in a chair to observe the sick child. This type of recommendation is rare.

Q: Do I change anything if my child is sick?

A: If illness occurs during the day, you have time to determine how much medical intervention may be needed. Perhaps there may be a call to the pediatrician. The evening routine will then be planned and discussed.

Nighttime is different. If your child comes to you with complaints of feeling sick, determine if any of the following symptoms (or combinations) are present: fever, cough, rash, breathing difficulty, severe neck or abdominal pain, or diarrhea. You may decide to call the pediatrician for consultation, or observe your child over the course of the night.

Whatever action might be needed, your child should not be taken to your bed. Medically, this is not indicated; psychologically this is contraindicated.

Q: What do I do if my child comes to my room saying she has to throw up?

A: Take the obligatory trip to the bathroom with her. If vomiting does not occur right away, help your child get back to her bed. She can always come and get you if she really does get sick. Apart from that, if there is a vomiting episode, help her to get cleaned up and into bed to complete her bedtime routine as usual.

Whatever action might be needed, your child should *not* be taken to your bed. If this becomes a nightly occurrence, rule out any medical problem. If there is none, simply reinforce the bedtime rule the same way you would as if your child routinely came to your bedroom after her bedtime (see FAQ: What do we do when our child keeps knocking on the door?).

Q: We discover that our child is reading long after he goes to bed. Is this okay?

A: If your child appears healthy and alert during the day, he is probably getting enough sleep. To keep things consistent, add a "lights out" clause to the rule (In bed for the night at 9:00, lights out at 9:30).

Q: We have just started What's the Rule? for bedtime; now our son is up at night having tantrums and, therefore, is getting less sleep. We got a note from the teacher stating that he is falling asleep in class. What should we do?

A: Make an appointment to talk with his teacher or send a note. Explain that you are starting a new rule to help your child develop a better bedtime routine and that over the next few days there may be some bumps in the road. Assure her that this will not be a problem for more than a week, and probably for only a couple more days. Ask the teacher to bear with it, as you are "on it" and are convinced that your child will benefit in alertness, mood, and obedience in the long run.

Q: What if my child comes into the room asking for a drink or other similar requests?

A: It sounds like you have an open-door policy. Consider changing it.

Whenever your child comes into your room at night, turn on a light and sit up, then ask, "What's the rule?" Generally, this routine will solve the problem. If your child hesitates leaving the room, get up, walk to the door, beckon her to come to you, and then give the nonverbal gesture of going back to her room. The purpose of going to the door and beckoning your child is used because a child is more likely to *come* to a parent than to *leave* a parent (who is in bed).

If the problem comes up a second time, have the meeting, and talk about the requests. Take a problem-solving approach with your child—however, always end with a clear rule. For example, when children seem to require water after they are in bed, a solution usually is to allow your child to put a glass of water beside the bed *before* bedtime.

Q: What about the bad effects of sleep loss if my child makes a fuss when we start the new rule?

A: There are some myths about sleep loss. Some parents are fearful that their child will become ill (highly unlikely) or will perform poorly in school the following day (that is possible). There are a couple of things to consider here. First, establishing What's the Rule? for bedtime is usually fully accomplished in three to seven nights. Usually, each night everyone gets a bit more sleep. Second, in contrast, previously troubled bedtimes were continually stressful for both child and parents, which not only fails to promote good health but also fails to promote good attention or good behavior.

Q: How do I handle special events that require us to stay out late?

A: Special events will occasionally come up; they are a part of life. All special nighttime activities should be planned at least 24 hours in advance. Springing a nighttime event on a child who is trying to learn some basic rules and who needs consistency is going to set back your efforts. Typical events may be as simple as a visit to a relative's house for dinner or less predictable, as in a baseball game that goes into extra innings. The day before the event, sit down with your child and explain the event (which he hopefully already knows about) and how the rule will be affected. Explain that the routine will be the same, just later at night. Keeping the routine the same (i.e., brushing teeth, showering, getting on pajamas, reading a story, etc.) preserves much of the rule and tends to be calming to your child, thus promoting sleep.

Some parents think, "My child is up too late as it is, so it is best to skip the bedtime routine and just put him right to bed." The additional 15-30 minutes of staying up to complete the routine will help your child to prepare for sleep and to have the consistency of the routine. It will also help your child stay on track for the following night.

Q: Can my child have a sleepover?

A: Of course. However, do not expect your child to maintain any aspect of her bedtime routine. Make sure that all the kids sleep within the same room and that they bring sleeping bags or blankets and pillows, so that there is at least a chance that they will eventually fall asleep. Sleepovers have a longstanding tradition of excitement, independence, and sleep loss; just get back into the routine the next day.

Q: What if my child has a sleepover at someone else's house?

A: Sleepovers at homes of non-family members are an important part of development. I encourage them.

Things that occur at other people's houses are out of your control. The assumption is that you know the other family well and that the children are safe. You may prepare your child by letting him know that What's the Rule? will not happen at his friend's (he probably knows this!). In your home, there is a good night rule; in his friend's home, there is not.

Parents often tell me that they don't like sleepovers, because their child comes home a bit "unruly," (interesting term, when you think about it.) The fun of a sleepover is the very *lack* of rules! Your child's feeling of independence may be greatly enhanced by this exciting experience, but she will need a little time to readjust—like all of us when we return from a stimulating social event or even a vacation. Be patient, be considerate (the kid probably got a maximum of two hour's sleep!) but be consistent; it will pass in an hour or two.

Q: What if my child ends up sleeping on the couch?

A: This is similar to the problem referred to in the question about the child sleeping on the floor in front of the parents' room. When your child falls asleep anywhere other than her bed, turn on the lights and gently wake her. It is tempting and easier to just carry a smaller child to bed—but resist. This encourages the "miracle of the morning"—waking up in a bed that your child didn't get to on his own. It delays success with the What's the Rule? technique.

If this problem continues beyond three days of your waking him, hold the meeting and tell your child that you will be installing something on his door (chimes, bell, etc.) that will help remind him about the rule (and help you wake up to quickly reinforce the rule). The learning curve won't be as long if you can ask "What's the rule?" as soon as possible upon your child leaving his bedroom.

Q: Our child gets up during the night and raids the kitchen. What can we do about this?

A: Nighttime snacking is one of the more resistant habits to alter—for two reasons. The behavior may be driven by hunger—although not always—and the behavior usually occurs when the parents are sleeping.

First, in all cases of secret eating, which may include hoarding under the bed or other places, have your pediatrician check your child, because certain types of driven hunger and snacking may indicate a medical condition—although rarely. Once this is ruled out, the following courses of action will turn things around.

There are two phases of intervention; if you are lucky, you'll never have to go beyond phase one.

Phase one: As always, start with the meeting. Express two concerns—one, your child leaving the room and two, your child raiding the kitchen. In the conversation, tell your child that you understand that he may be hungry during the night.

Take a problem solving approach with your child—however, always end up with a clear rule. As far as snacks are concerned, to avoid spills and crumbs throughout the house, it's best to limit any household eating to the kitchen or dining room. A snack can occur in the kitchen before bedtime teeth brushing.

Phase two: Let's say that your child continues to raid the kitchen. Don't despair; this is a tough problem. In phase two, you will have to "secure" the kitchen and the food. Usually, this is as simple as locking the kitchen door. If your house is constructed so that this is not possible, then lock some cupboards and the refrigerator at night. A locksmith can install locks that only show the key plate and are not an eyesore.

Because it may take a few days to install locks, this is a good time to have the meeting to explain what you are doing. As always, take a kind approach, saying that you are doing this because it is an extra step in helping your child to remember the rule on his own: "If you forget the rule and see that the door is locked, you can say to yourself, 'Oh, gosh; I forgot What's the Rule?' and go back to bed."

After a few days, hold another meeting, and talk to your child about the idea of giving another try at having the kitchen door or cupboards unlocked for a night. The idea here is to constantly give your child an opportunity for success; locking the doors is meant only as a temporary cue for a lifetime of habit change.

Q: My child needs to have the TV on in order to fall asleep. Is this bad?

TV sets in bedrooms are way of life—unfortunately! However, the use of them requires rules. Many children who say they "cannot sleep without the TV on" have parents who sympathize with this point of view because they, too, had this habit as a child (and still do). However, I don't recommend it. If you live in a noisy neighborhood and need to mask sounds, consider an inexpensive white noise machine. We've used them in our waiting room to mask the sound of talk coming from our offices.

Often the TV postpones or interrupts rather than encourages sleep. It requires volume adjustment, program monitoring, and turning on and off. As nighttime progresses, programs and commercials become less and less appropriate and do not promote good sleep.

Simply add to the bedtime rule: "TV off at bedtime."

Q: What do we do when we go on a vacation?

It is almost impossible to preserve bedtime rules during vacation. Talk about the vacation at the meeting. Point out that there may be day-to-day adjustments (actually night to night) about bedtime; and that each morning the family will go over the plans and bedtime.

Although the time of going to bed may vary, whenever you can, preserve the home routine (bath, pajamas, story, etc.). Naturally, avoid having children share your bed. That will present big problems when you get home. Sharing beds with siblings and sharing rooms may be unavoidable. If the vacation is at the home of a relative or friend, be sure you know the sleeping arrangements ahead of time. If they are less than ideal, at least you can discuss this with your children before you leave.

Have the mindset that after vacation the original rules will be back in place. Just make sure that they are! For the first night or two at home, you may feel as though you are starting all over again. Take heart, you're not. By calmly and kindly adhering to What's the Rule? everybody will get back on track, usually in 24 hours.

Q: My child goes back to his bedroom but screams and breaks things. What can I do?

A: This is one of the more extreme cases. We see it most often when there has been a long and unsuccessful history of trying different methods to change a child's bedtime behavior. In cases of what appears to be total disregard of the rule plus loud and destructive behavior, remember that that is not the end of the world (it only seems that way). It is an extreme form of testing behavior.

The destructive behavior is a merely a tantrum, dressed up in an ugly suit; ignore it no matter how spectacular or lengthy it is. Also ignore swearing, name calling, and any other attempts to get you off course. These are all red herrings. The destruction, as well as the problem with the rule, should be handled at the meeting the next morning. The bad language should be handled at another meeting. Keep it simple. Tantrums do play themselves out. They lessen in intensity and frequency more quickly when ignored.

The next morning, follow the meeting format, but with two additions. Let your child know that he will have to pick up his room before dinner (or before play, etc.) In brief, your child has dinner or play (or whatever) *after* the chore is finished. Resist the urge to pick up your child's room for him; it will only guarantee repeated tantrums.

In regard to destruction of property: destruction by your child of his own stuff is self-reinforcing as long as you don't replace the destroyed items. If he wants to do it, things may be glued or taped together by your child with minimal help from you.

Q: Our 8 year old still wets the bed sometimes. He comes to our door to ask for help with his wet pajamas and bed. How should we handle this?

A: This topic is big enough for a book all by itself. Assuming that there is no medical condition causing the problem, we'll focus only on the What's the Rule? part of it. A Good Night is all about your child learning to take care of himself at night, to feel self-confident, independent, and secure. Your focus with the bedwetting issue is still on the simple bedtime rule. However, bedwetting is a sensitive problem for children, most of whom feel shame about it. At the meeting, indicate that you have come up with a system to help your child follow the rule about bedtime (i.e., in bed at 9:00 for the whole night) while he is outgrowing the bedwetting. At bedtime, he will have a change of pajamas by the bed and dry bed covers to make himself comfortable. The rule remains the same.

THE END

INDEX

W

www.ingramcontent.com/pod-product-compliance
Lightning Source LLC
Chambersburg PA
CBHW021102090426
42738CB00006B/471